AF860250

A

DISCOURSE

CONCERNING

TREASONS,

AND

BILLS of Attainder.

Majeſtas Reipublicæ, eſt in quâ continetur Dignitas & Amplitudo Civitatis.— Et læſæ Majeſtatis Crimen eſt, Quum Majeſtas Minuatur. Tull. ad Heren. 1. & 4.

Licet etiam apud Concilium, accuſare quoque, & diſcrimen Capitis intendere.
Tac. de Mor. Ger.

THE LAWBOOK EXCHANGE, LTD.
Clark, New Jersey
2008

ISBN-13: 978-1-58477-698-7
ISBN-10: 1-58477-698-6

The quality of this reprint is equivalent to the quality of the original work.

The Lawbook Exchange, Ltd.
33 Terminal Avenue
Clark, New Jersey 07066-1321

Please see our website for a selection of our other publications and fine facsimile reprints of classic works of legal history:
www.lawbookexchange.com

Library of Congress Cataloging-in-Publication Data

West, Richard, d. 1726.
A discourse concerning treasons, and bills of attainder / Richard West.
p. cm.
Originally published: London, J. Roberts, 1716.
Includes bibliographical references.
ISBN-13: 978-1-58477-698-7 (alk. paper)
ISBN-10: 1-58477-698-6 (alk. paper)
1. Treason--Great Britain. 2. Inheritance and succession--Great Britain. 3. Land tenure--Law and legislation--Great Britain I. Title.
KD8022.W474 2005
345.41'0231--dc22 2006005523

Printed in the United States of America on acid-free paper

A

DISCOURSE

CONCERNING

TREASONS,

AND

BILLS of Attainder.

Majestas Reipublicæ, est in quâ continetur Dignitas & Amplitudo Civitatis.— Et læsæ Majestatis Crimen est, Quum Majestas Minuatur. Tull. ad Heren. 1. & 4.

Licet etiam apud Concilium, accusare quoque, & discrimen Capitis intendere. Tac. de Mor. Ger.

LONDON:

Printed for J. ROBERTS, near the *Oxford-Arms* in *Warwick-Lane.* 1716.

Price One Shilling and Six-pence.

THE

CONTENTS.

The

The CONTENTS.

A DIS-

A DISCOURSE Concerning Treasons, &c.

THE regular and impartial Adminiſtration of Juſtice, as it is the *chief End* for which Government was at firſt inſtituted; ſo it is the only Means by which it can be long preſerved. For whenever a Failure of it happens, either by the Weakneſs or Corruption of its Miniſters; it throws a State into ſuch Convulſions, as generally end in Ruin. The moſt conſiderable

Branch of publick Juſtice, is that which relates to the *Puniſhment of Offenders*; ſince it is that which gives an additional Weight and Sanction, even to its Deciſions of another nature; and it is the *Fear of that only*, which retains the greateſt Part of Mankind from committing thoſe Diſorders, which would render all Society intolerable.

Before the *Report from the Secret Committee* was printed, the Friends of the late Miniſtry contented themſelves with denying that they were guilty of any Crime; and ſo long as there was not any demonſtrative Evidence of their Guilt, they had Credit enough, even upon that foot, to maintain the Spirit of their Party: But ſince that *Report* is publiſhed, they have been forced to give the Diſpute a new Turn, of a much more *dangerous nature*. They do not now pretend to affirm their Actions juſtifiable; they, to a Man, all condemn their Procedure in every particular; yet, from I know not what kind of Principle, they are wonderfully induſtrious and zealous, to argue the World into a Belief, that by reaſon of ſome Defects in the Forms of Law, ſome *imaginary Flaws* in our Conſtitution, the People of *Great Britain* have not a Right, by their Repreſentatives in Parliament, of demanding any Capital Puniſhment to be inflicted upon them.

That ſome particular Perſons related to the Criminals, or Partakers with them in their Crimes, ſhould lay down Propoſitions of this nature, is not ſurprizing: But that a numerous Body of Men, profeſſing a Zeal for their Country, and a ſteddy Loyalty to the *preſent King*, ſhould be capable of reaſoning themſelves into it, is amazing. For is it poſſible, that a Society of many Millions ſhould not have that Right, which no ſingle private Man can ever be ſuppoſed to be without? Can a Nation be ever reduced to ſuch Circumſtances, as to be deprived of the Uſe of ſuch Means, as are abſolutely neceſſary to its Preſervation? It is a moſt infallible Maxim, that in a Country *where nothing is puniſhed, every thing will be attempted.* And yet this is the Caſe to which theſe People would bring the Government: So ſtrongly are they attach'd to the Intereſts of a Party, that they chooſe rather to ſacrifice the Law, than ſurrender up their Leaders to Juſtice. For it is Nonſenſe to talk of Laws and Conſtitution, if any Man may commit what is notoriouſly moſt prejudicial to his Country, and yet eſcape with Impunity by ſcreening himſelf behind Formalities. Such an evaſive Tranſgreſſion of the Law, inſtead of juſtifying the Criminal, ſhould, by all the Rules of common Senſe, enhance his Guilt; ſince it neceſſarily implies him to be conſcious, that what he did was illegal and unwarrantable. In short, all Forms of Law, and I may odd *Statutes*, relating to the Adjudication or Trial of *Treasons*, were intended as *Barriers to the Liberties of the People* against the Incroachments of the Crown, and not to protect corrupt Ministers from the Prosecutions of Parliament.

As the Design of this Paper is not particularly to examine the Conduct of the late Ministry, I shall not say much concerning them, but refer the Reader to the *Report* from the *Committee of Secrecy*, in which all their Actions seem to be represented in their proper Light. What I propose, is, to consider the Arguments which are made use of to prevent their Punishment. I do not mean those, which are urg'd by Persons who can still say, they think their Actions entirely justifiable; but such as, allowing their Actions to be highly criminal, and prejudicial to their Country in general, yet warmly oppose their being punished capitally; by reason, say they, that what they did is not within the express Letter of any Law, &c.

The Substance of what they alledge amounts to this; That the Uncertainty of *Treason* at the Common Law being by Experience found to be a great Grievance, an *Act of Parliament* was made *Anno* 25° E. 3. to remedy it; by which all *Treasons*

are

are reduc'd and limited to the particular Cases mentioned in that *Statute*. That this *Statute* ought to be observ'd and kept sacred, it having met with the constant Approbation of every Age since it has been made, and having been confirm'd by several subsequent *Acts of Parliament*.

They own indeed, that there is a Clause in the *Act*, by which the Parliament did reserve to themselves and Successors, the Power of declaring any other Case to be *Treason*, which might happen in Time to come. But then they positively affirm, that Clause of Reservation to be repeal'd by the 1° *H*. 4. *Cap*. 14. and 1° *Mar. Reg. Cap*. 1, *&c.* And that therefore nothing can now be said or declared to be Treason, but what is plainly express'd to be such in the 25° *E*. 3. or some other subsequent *Statute*.

It is not, say they, the Case of these particular Persons, which is to be so much considered: The Law ought to be sacredly observed; and People ought not, in order to punish a few Criminals, tho' of the deepest Guilt, make such Precedents, as may be of perpetual Prejudice to the Liberties of *Britain*. They will readily agree, that the Actions of the late Ministry were as contrary to the true Interest of their Country, as possible; but it not appearing by the *Report*, that what they did is *Treason*, within the expreſs Words of that *Statute*, or of any other, they cannot agree to their being puniſh'd as Traytors: *Not becauſe they do not think them criminal, but becauſe the Law is defective.*

And farther, as to any Proceedings againſt them by way of *Bill of Attainder*, as it is what they are moſt apprehenſive of, ſo is it what they clamour the moſt againſt; aſſerting all ſuch *Bills* to be in their own Nature unjuſt: For, ſay they, the Law of *England* is every Man's Inheritance, and let him be never ſo criminal, it is always unjuſt to deprive him of the Privilege and Protection of it. It is the Law that is the Rule of every Man's Actions, and that determines them to be either juſt or unjuſt: Every Man therefore has reaſon to conclude all his Actions to be (if not juſtifiable) at leaſt unpuniſhable, ſo long as the Law does not take hold of them. So that, ſay they, all Acts of Attainder muſt neceſſarily be either uſeleſs and impertinent, or highly wicked and unjuſt: For every Man's Actions, if they are within the Extent of the Law, are puniſhable in the ordinary Courſe of it; and if they are not, *a Bill of Attainder* is *a Judgment ex poſt facto*, puniſhing the Perſon for Actions, which he had all the Reaſon in the World, to think himſelf ſafe in doing.

This

This Language and Way of Reaſoning is certainly very proper for ſuch Perſons, who openly profeſs themſelves to be againſt the Proſecution of the late Miniſtry in any manner whatſoever, and who perhaps at the bottom are ſo thoroughly their Friends, that they think the *only Fault* in their Schemes and Deſigns to be *their want of Succeſs*. And without doubt, the great Heat they ſhew in their Defence, is much more juſtifiable under this plauſible Pretence of a Veneration for the Laws and Conſtitution, than it would be, did they openly avow an Approbation of all the late Tranſactions. And I am apt enough to believe, that if we were able to diſcern Perſons and Things in their proper Light, we ſhould find this alone to be the true Spring and Cauſe of all this ſtrange *ex tempore Zeal* in ſeveral of thoſe very Perſons, who upon other Occaſions have been the foremoſt to trample upon that very Conſtitution they would now ſeem to defend.

But however weak and fallacious theſe Arguments are, and how viſible ſoever it is, that they are only made uſe of to ſerve their Cauſe in this critical Juncture of Affairs; yet have they deceived many well-meaning Perſons, who being always in earneſt themſelves, when they talk of the Law and Conſtitution, think that all others are ſo too; and by that means they are frequently drawn in to be subservient and assistant to such Designs, and to protect such Persons, as they most abhor. So long as the Dispute was wholly political, as whether this or that Scheme was the more eligible, *&c.* I own I did not think my self, or any other private Person, to be much concern'd: But when they carried Matters so far, as to argue, that notwithstanding they shou'd be criminal, yet they were *so dextrously criminal*, the Law had not Force sufficient to punish them: The first time I heard this Notion, it shock'd my Reason. It introduces such an unaccountable Weakness and Incapacity into the very original Frame of our Constitution, that the Government (if this Doctrine be true) is not able to support it self any longer than the *very worst Man, subject to it, will vouchsafe to permit.*

I immediately endeavour'd to examine, as far as I was able, the Laws concerning Treason, to see whether our Constitution labours under those Flaws and Defects, which they assert it does. And if the uninterrupted Practice of Parliaments is a sufficient Evidence of what our Ancestors esteemed as Law in Parliament; then, till better informed, must I think, that such Persons as are guilty of the Crimes charged from the Report of the Secret Committee, *are by the Law of* England *punishable as Traytors*;

And

And that the proceeding againſt any Perſon by way of *Bill of Attainder*, for Actions, which are Treaſons by the Common Law, and which are not ſpecified to be ſuch in any Statute, is not only juſt, but legal, and even in ſome Caſes abſolutely neceſſary to preſerve our Conſtitution: and that it has been the conſtant Practice of Parliaments. In order therefore to make this clear and evident, I ſhall,

I. Examine what was the true and antient Notion of Treaſon at the Common-Law, and what was the Practice of our Anceſtors in Parliament until the Statute of 25 *E.* 3. was made.

II. I ſhall then conſider what Alteration that or any other Statute has made upon the Common Law, and what has been the Practice of our Anceſtors ſubſequent to it.

I. The Word *Treaſon* properly ſignifies a betraying, and therefore cannot be committed, but where ſome Truſt is repoſed. *Britton*, *p.* 16. ſays that it is " *Cheſcun damage que lon fait a ſcient, ou procure de faire, a que lon fait amy.* It is every Damage, " which any Man knowingly does or procures to be done to another, to whom he " pretends to be a Friend. So that in this Senſe every Man who acts contrary to any

Obli-

Obligation he is under, may be ſaid to commit a Treaſon, (*i. e.*) to betray or deceive the Perſon who is the Object of it, who muſt neceſſarily be ſuppoſed to have plac'd a Confidence in his Performance, ſince he had a Right to exact it. And therefore it is eſſential to the Notion of Treaſon, that there ſhould be ſome moral Relation between the Parties; Which is either natural, as between *Father and Son*, &c. or contracted, as between *Lord and Tenant*, &c.

This was the old and original Senſe of the Word; and it was a conſiderable Time before it came to be appropriated to the Senſe we now uſe it in. At firſt, almoſt every Breach of Truſt was comprehended under it; but now Cuſtom has entirely altered and changed it, ſo as to make it ſignify only ſome certain Species of *Breaches of Truſt of the higheſt Nature.*

Andrew Horn, an Author who lived either in the Reign of *Ed.* 1 or 2. never makes uſe of the Word Treaſon, to expreſs any Crime committed againſt either King or Kingdom. Tho' it is manifeſt that the acting contrary to thoſe Obligations which every Man is under to the Publick, is within the general Definition of the Word. But in his Diviſion of Crimes he makes two diſtinct Chapters of *Crimes of Majeſty*, and *Crimes of Treaſon.*

He

He diſtinguiſhes his Crimes altogether by the Object or the Perſon againſt whom they are committed, and defines the Crime of Majeſty to be an Offence done againſt the King. And in treating of it, he does not regard the different Heinouſneſs of Facts, but makes the Term ſo general as to include all Offences (almoſt) whatſoever, which are done againſt the King. For, ſays he, *e. g.* all thoſe who commit Perjury againſt the King fall into this Offence; as, *e. g.* the King's Miniſters, who are ſworn to do Juſtice, and forſwear themſelves in any particular. He enumerates a great number of Crimes of this and inferior Natures, all under the Denomination of *Majeſty*, ſome of which were ſtiled mortal Offences, and others not ſo. So that it ſeems (according to this Author) every Crime committed againſt the King or Publick, by reaſon of their Community of Object, was equally a Crime of Majeſty. But as all Crimes are not equal as to the Heinouſneſs of their Guilt, ſo the Puniſhment of theſe Crimes was to be inflicted *pro modo & ratione delicti*; the Adjudication of which was abſolutely in the Breaſt of the Judges, who were entirely at the Diſpoſition of the Crown.

The Term *Treaſon* he makes to be almoſt as general as that of *Majeſty*. Since he makes it include every other Crime, which

which implies the Breach of an Obligation, which may be contracted by *Blood*, *Affinity*, *Homage*, *Oath* or *Service*, *Vid. Mirror des Justices. Cap.* 1. § 4, 5, 7. The Term of Crime of Majesty is not now used in our Law, but is entirely sunk and lost, and the Division in Criminal Cases now in Use is, into *High Treason* and *Petit Treason.*

High Treason is defin'd to be an horrible Offence committed against the Security of either King or Kingdom, whether it be by Imagination, Word or Deed. Cowel's Interp. So that it includes all those Crimes of Majesty, which *Andrew Horn* styles mortal. *Petit Treason* is when a Wife kills her Husband, a Servant his Master, *&c.* and includes almost all those Capital Offences, which he places under the Title of Treason.

This Division of Treason into *Grand & Petit* is very antient. But then it was not used to signify precisely that Sense it does now. *Britton* makes no other Use of it than to distinguish those Crimes which were punished with Death, from those which were punished by Mutilation, Pillory, or any other inferiour Sort of Punishment. His Words are, *Cap.* 8. " *Et poit estre Treson grand & pettit dount ascun demande Jugement de Mort, & ascun Amission de Membre & Jugement de Pillori, ou penaunce de prison, & ascun pluis simple punishment solonques la manere del fait. Grand Tre-*

" *son*

" *ſon eſt a compaſſer noſtre Mort ou deſheriter*
" *nous de noſtre Royalmes*, &c. *Et ſi poit*
" *Homme faire Grand Treſon verſauters*
" *Perſons en moults maneres, comme en procu-*
" *rant la Mort de aſcun que eſt ſeiſi de luy*,
" &c. And Treaſon may be either High
" (Grand) or Petit; of which ſome de-
" mand Judgment of Death, and other
" ſome Mutilation, Judgment of Pillory
" or Impriſonment, and other ſome more
" ſimple Puniſhment, according to the Pro-
" portion of the Crime. High-Treaſon
" is to compaſs our Death, or to diſinherit
" us of our Realms, *&c.* And High-Trea-
" ſon may be committed againſt other
" Perſons in many Manners, as, *e. g.* If
" any Man ſhould procure the Death of
" any Perſon who is ſeiſed of him, *&c.*

§. It is evident to any Perſon who reads the ancient Books of the Law, that the Term Treaſon, as denoting a particular Species of Crimes, was of a very uncertain Senſe. It appears in ſome Meaſure by what has been before ſaid. And as it is not Words but Things that we enquire after, I ſhall not ſpend much Time in ſettling too critically their Senſe.

It is ſufficient to the Purpoſe of this Paper, if it can be ſhewn, that every Action of conſiderable Conſequence, which in Intendment of Law was look'd upon as prejudicial to the publick Society or Nation, on, as ſuch, and to have been done *animo lædendi*, has been always capitally puniſh'd; puniſh'd even as it is at this Day, by loſs of Life, and Forfeiture of all Eſtate Real and Perſonal, *&c.*

It matters not by what Name it has been called, whether *Crime of Majeſty*, or *Treaſon*, or *Felony*, &c. For whatever Action we can ſhew to have been puniſhed in ſo ſevere a Manner, I think we may without ſcruple ſtile *High Treaſon*, even in the Modern Senſe of the Word. The *Saxons* had no Notion of any other Treaſon, than that of Treachery to their Country, and deſerting it in Time of Danger. They puniſhed it with Death as ſoon as ever they diſcovered it; and even in their Supreme Councils, or to ſpeak in the Language of the preſent Age, in their Parliaments, they took Cognizance of Crimes of this Nature, and as it were, attainted the Criminals. *Tacitus* ſays, " *Licet apud concilium accuſare quo-* " *que & diſcrimen Capitis intendere*, and " then adds, *Proditores & transfugas Ar-* " *boribus ſuſpendunt*. Vid. de Mor. Germa. C. 12. p. 609.

They brought theſe Notions with them from *Germany* into *England*; and it has been but very lately queſtion'd, *Whether a Man could betray his Country without being a Traytor.*

Their

Their Laws (here in *England*) were remarkably Merciful, and few Crimes were among them punish'd with Death: So that doubtless those which were so, were such as they look'd upon with the utmost Horror and Detestation. The killing of any Person was in general Terms made Capital in their Laws. But then there was a Commutation allow'd of, which was regulated in proportion to the Value of the Head, or Life of the Person who was kill'd. The very killing of their *King* was not among them punished with Death, provided the Criminal was able to produce a certain Sum of Money. The Valuation of Peoples Lives in this manner, was a Thing so fixed and certain among them, that it was grown a part of their Common Law, as may appear by the Laws of King *Athelstane*, *p.* 55. " *Inter leg.* Saxon. *ad Calc.* Bede *Regij*, *Ca-* " *pitis Estimatio*, Jure Anglorum Communi, " *Triginta Thrymsarum millibus constat.*" Which is just twice the Sum the Life of an Archbishop, or any other Nobleman, was valued at: And therefore in the Law before mentioned, it is added, by way of Reason for it, " *Quorum quindecem Millia,* " *capitis estimationis, reliqua Regni nomine* " *debentur; hæc ad gentem, illa ad cognatos* " *pertinent.*" This Money, which was paid upon any Person's being kill'd, was distributed among the Relations of the deceased, to satisfie them for their Loss. And the only Reason which can be collected from their Law, why the Life of their King was valued at double the Sum of another Nobleman, is that great Interest which the Publick has in the Preservation of the Prince: And their Loss being at least equal to that of his Family; the Commutation Money was therefore equally divided between them.

This was the Value the antient *Saxons* put upon their Kings, at the same Time that Crimes of really much less Consequence to the Society were punished with Death, *&c.* *Inter ejusdem* Athelst. leg. p. 47. " *Si quis Domino suo Calamitatem* " *struxisse accusetur, neque id legitime poterit* " *inficiari, capitale esto. Inter leg.* Canuti, p. 121. " *Cædes manifestæ, Dominorumque* " *proditiones, scelera sunt Jure humano in-* " *expiabilia.*" So that it seems no Commutation was allowed for these Crimes. In short, it may fairly be concluded, that what we now call High Treason, cou'd not among them be committed, but only against the Publick; since their severest Punishments were only pointed at such Crimes, which had the Publick, as such, for their Object. As a farther Proof of which, I shall recite one *Saxon* Law more. *Inter leges* Canuti, p. 125. " *Si quis in Terrestri sive* " *Navali pugna Dominum suum* (so the Word is translated by *Lambard*, but the

Saxon

Saxon Word is *gorefan*, and properly signifies, *a Leader in War*) "*aut commilitonem suum per ignaviam & pigritiam deseruerit, vitâ & rebus suis omnibus mulctator, & quem illi prius dederat fundum Dominus recipito, sin quæ ex scripto* (*boclande*) *prædia possederit, ea Regi sunto.*" This is as it were, the very Judgment which is now given in Cases of Treason; and there cannot be any Reason assigned why so great a Punishment was inflicted upon such a Crime (as in the Times we now live, is scarcely counted any) but only that vast Interest which the Publick has in every private Man's fully discharging his Duty in Battles, *&c.* and Circumstances of that Nature.

Indeed upon *Canutus*'s consenting to dismiss his *Danish* Army, a Law was made for the farther Security of his Person, in some measure to recompence him for the Loss of his Troops; by which an Attempt upon his Person was made Capital without any Commutation, *Pag.* 120. "*Si quis saluti Regis aut Domini sui insidias tetenderit, vitâ & rebus suis omnibus plectitor, nisi quidem triplicis ordalii questione crimen diluerit.* This Law was a *perfect Novelty to the Saxons*; to prove which, and also to prevent the Reader's imagining the Commutation, in case of killing the King, was only allowed where it was done by Accident, I shall recite this Law of King *Alured*,

Pag. 24. "*Qui capiti & ſaluti Regis perfidioſè, ſive ſolus, ſive ſervis aut ſicariis mercede conductis, ſtipatus inſidiabitur, vitâ & fortunis ejus omnibus privator; verùm ſi is ſe culpâ eximere voluerit, æſtimationis Regii Capitis ratione habitâ, id facito.*

It is obſerved by a late Learned Writer, out of the *Mirror of Juſtice*, p. 75. That among the *Saxons*, Plotting againſt the King, was but Felony: And upon the ſuppoſed Authority of that Book, he refers to an Indictment in King *Alfred*'s Time, for an Offence of that nature, as concluding only *felonicè*; whereas Indictments in the other Caſe concluded always *felonicè & proditoriè*. And he obſerves that the Puniſhment of the one was Loſs of Life, and Forfeiture of Perſonal Eſtate only; of the other, Loſs of Life, with Forfeiture of the whole Eſtate, both Real and Perſonal.

I ſhall only make a ſhort Remark upon this Notion, and then haſten to the Time of the *Normans*, as being much more material towards the ſettling the Queſtion now in hand. It is ſcarcely probable, that the Term *Felony* was in uſe among the *Saxons*, in a Senſe any thing like what it is now among us; it is not to be found in all the *Saxon* Laws extant. The Word is of a moſt general Senſe, and Sir *Henry Spelman*'s Definition of it is certainly true, "*Felo-*

" *nia*

" *nia est culpa seu injuria propter quam Vas-*
" *salus amittit feudum.* The Etymology of the Word expresses this Sense; for it may be derived from the *Saxon* Word *(Felen)* to mistake, to commit a Crime, *&c.* or else from the Word *(Feah)* which signifies Money, Wages, and even an Inheritance, and *(Lon)* which in the *German* Tongue signified a Price. It is visible that Treason is within this Sense of the Word, as much as any other Crime, which creates a Forfeiture: For as to the different Conclusions of the Indictments, *felonicè*, or *felonicè & proditoriè*, it seems to be an Observation founded wholly upon modern Practice. And whoever reads Dr. *Hickes*'s *Dissertatio Epistolaris in Thesaur. Ling. Septent.* will easily believe, that the Pleadings and Acts of Court among the *Saxons* were not in *Latin*. He recites several Acts of several County-Courts, as of *Hereford*, *&c.* every one of them in the *Saxon* Language. It was a considerable time before the Word *Felony* was used in so precise a Sense, as it is now; and High Treason was frequently comprehended under it, even since the Conquest. It is certain from both *Glanvill* and *Britton*, that *Falsifying the Great Seal* was High Treason at the Common Law; and yet *M.* 1. *E.* 3. *Pl.* 13. a Man being arraigned for having falsified the Great Seal, pleaded a Charter of Pardon *de touts Felonyes*; and

it was allowed him. As to what is obſerved concerning the Difference of the Judgments, it is a manifeſt Error; ſince, among the *Saxons*, the Puniſhment of *Murthers*, *Burglaries*, *Robberies*, *&c.* was commuted for a certain Sum of Money, which they call'd *Weregild*: And this Law continued until the Reign of *Hen.* 1. by whom it was abrogated. " *Et is primum ſuſpen-" dium furibus indixit. Vid. Floren. Wigorn. pag.* 653. *& Roger Hoveden inter Scriptores poſt Bedam, pag.* 471.

The *Normans* with great Juſtice improv'd upon the Laws of the *Saxons*: They conſider'd the *Crown* as the *Center*, in which all the Members of the Commonwealth were united and knit together: And an Attempt upon the Perſon of the Prince cou'd not be look'd upon but as tending to diſſolve that *Union*, and conſequently to reduce the State into Confuſion; therefore was it made equally capital with thoſe Crimes, which related only to the Kingdom. And this appears by all the old Books. *Glanv. lib.* 14. " *Accuſatore in Curiâ probante certiſſimè,* " *ſe ſciviſſe ipſum accuſatum machinatum fu-* " *iſſe, vel aliquid feciſſe, in mortem Regis,* " *vel ſeditionem Regni, &c.* Bracton, lib. 3. pag. 118. " *Si quis auſu temerario machi-* " *natus ſit in mortem Domini Regis, vel ali-* " *quid egerit, ſeu agi procuraverit, ad ſedi-* " *tionem Domini Regis vel Exercitus ſui, &c.*

It

It is to be obſerved, that *Bracton* did not intend this for an entire Definition of Treaſon, ſince he juſt before uſes theſe Words: "*Habet enim crimen leſæ Majeſtatis ſub ſe* "*multas ſpecies, quarum una hæc eſt, ut ſi* "*quis*, &c. *Fleta*, lib. 1. pag. 31. ſays, "*Quiſquis ſit de crimine leſæ Majeſtatis ac-* "*cuſatus, defendere ſe debet ſic; omnem felo-* "*niam defendit, omnemque ſubductionem Re-* "*gis, Regni, vel ſui Exercitûs*, &c. *Hen-* "*gham magna*, cap. 1. pag. 7. "*Conſtat* "*quòd placita de crimine leſæ Majeſtatis,* "*ut de Nece vel Seditione* Perſonæ *Domini* "*Regis, vel Regni, vel Exercitûs*, &c. *ad* "*Curiam Regis majorem pertinent*, &c. By theſe Quotations, and what has been before ſaid, it appears that the *Normans* coupled Crimes againſt the publick Safety, and againſt the Perſons of their Princes, together: And indeed in Reaſon it is not poſſible to ſeparate them; for as the Murther, *&c.* of a King, muſt neceſſarily involve a State in Confuſion, ſo every Action which endangers the Safety of the Publick, muſt neceſſarily diminiſh the Majeſty of the Prince. And this may be eſteemed a juſt Reaſon, why all Crimes of this nature are by Intendment ſaid to be committed *contra Coronam & Dignitatem Regis*. The very Term, *King*, bears a neceſſary and indiſſoluble Relation to a Kingdom; and therefore the Safety, *&c.* of a People muſt be the chief Intereſt of every *King*, as ſuch. And the Crown or Prince always proſecutes Crimes of this nature (perhaps) becauſe the Crown, as has been ſaid, is always conſidered as the Center of Union, and as it were the ſingle Principle of *Activity* in the Society.

It is not difficult to believe, that Judges, &c. who were entirely at the Diſpoſition of the King, ſhould be more zealous in the Proſecution of ſuch Crimes, which particularly affected the Intereſt or Perſon of the *Prince*, than of thoſe which related immediately to the *Publick*, *as ſuch*, and were very often diſtinct from, nay ſometimes perfectly oppoſite to, what a weak *Prince* might by the Advice of a *corrupt Miniſtry* look upon to be his Intereſt.

Their carrying this Principle on with too high a Hand, made it become a very great Grievance to the People, and was the true Reaſon of the Enacting the Act of 25° *Ed.* 3. *de Proditionibus*, as will be more particularly ſhewn, when we come to conſider that Statute.

1. What I ſhall now in the firſt place endeavour to ſhew, is, that before 25 *Ed.* 3. was made, the Parliament did take upon them to puniſh ſuch Crimes, which were committed againſt the Safety of the Publick, as Treaſon. And I preſume no Man will deny, that Cuſtom, which is the *Law* of Parlia-

Parliaments, is as much the *Law* of the Land, as any thing that has been the conſtant and uninterrupted Doctrine and Practice of *Weſtminſter-Hall*: For whatſoever is the *Law* of the Kingdom, is as much *Law*, as any thing elſe that is ſo; and whatſoever is *Law* cannot *ſuſcipere magis aut minus*, but it muſt be all of equal Authority. *Vid. Vaugh. pag.* 21. *& alibi.* In order to this, let us examine how our Anceſtors behav'd themſelves in reſpect to Miniſters, whom they felt to be the Plagues and Scourges of their Country; and I doubt not but upon the Iſſue it will appear, that *Treaſon*, by the Law of *England* in Parliament, is exactly what the Civil Law defines it to be; *ſcil. Quodcunque quis fuerit molitus contra Imperatorem vel Rempublicam, crimen eſt Majeſtatis.* Vinii Inſt. pag. 883. Forms of Law, and Niceties in the Proof of Facts, which they all experimentally knew to be true, did not hinder them from doing themſelves that Juſtice, which every *injured People* have a Right *to exact*; and which is abſolutely neceſſary to preſerve a Nation from the Inſults and Oppreſſions of Miniſters, who by their Intereſt and Credit with their Sovereign raiſe themſelves above the Fear of Puniſhment in the ordinary and common Proceedings of the Law.

I ſhall not in my Citation of Precedents go beyond thoſe Times, of which we have

Records extant. The common Hiſtorians, it is true, give us an Account of ſeveral Perſons who died as Traytors in different Reigns; but there not being any Records, whereby we might indiſputably demonſtrate the Truth of ſuch Hiſtories, a great many Perſons would perhaps think their Authority too weak a Foundation to build upon, in the Examination of a Point in Law of ſo great Conſequence as this.

The Reign of *Ed.* 2. will it ſelf furniſh us with Inſtances ſufficient of the Vigour and Bravery of our Anceſtors. Let it not be objected, as it has often been to the Reign of *Rich.* 2. *&c.* that the Times were in great Confuſion, and therefore Things were not then carried regularly, and according to the Forms of Law: For when ſhou'd we expect to find Precedents of *Parliamentary Juſtice* upon Miniſters who were guilty of Treaſons againſt the Publick, and perhaps were ſupported by wrong and *dangerous* Notions of *Prerogative*; but in thoſe only Times which *can poſſibly afford them?* When good and wiſe Princes govern'd, how cou'd there be any Diſpute between *Court* and *Parliament?* But when wicked Miniſters *ſeduc'd their Sovereigns* into dangerous and illegal Meaſures, it was then only that *Parliaments* could exert themſelves in *Vindication* of their *Liberties!* When Princes *defended* their Favourites

from

from the Juſtice of the Nation, it is then, and then only, it can be expected that *Parliaments* ſhould aſſert their Authority, and reſolve to do themſelves Juſtice! When that has been obtain'd, the Confuſions ceaſed, and Things have naturally return'd into their legal and accuſtomed Channel.

The Judgments which were given againſt *Gaveſton*, and the two *Spencers*, have been approved as juſt in every ſucceeding Age; and yet were their Caſe to be try'd according to the Principles which are now contended for, it would be found very difficult to convict them of any Crime worthy of Death. *Peter de Gaveſton* was a debauched flagitious Perſon, who for his Miſdemeanours, and corrupting Prince *Edward*, (with whom he was educated) was *Anno* 1306, & *Regn. Ed.* 1. 33. in Parliament baniſh'd the Kingdom, *de communi Aſſenſu procerum.* But this King was no ſooner dead, and the Crown deſcended to *Ed.* 2. than he was recall'd from his Exile, and before he could return home, the King even prevented his Wiſhes, with the greateſt Grant that *ever* was made to a Subject. The King himſelf, ſo haſty was he to ſhew his Affection to his Favorite could not ſtay for his Return from *Scotland*, where he was when the King his Father dy'd, but by Letters Patents, which are dated *apud Dumfreis*, 6 *Aug. Anno Regn.* 1. he granted to him and

and his Heirs the whole County of *Cornwall*. *Vid. Rymer's Fœd. Tom.* 3. *p.* 1. His excessive Grants were objected to *Gaveston* as a Crime; and yet the Letters Patents of this very Grant (which was by far the greatest) were witnessed and attested by the prime Nobility of the Kingdom. For they are, *Cum hiis testibus, Henrico de Lacy Com. Lincoln, Thoma Com. Lancastri, the Kings Uncle*, and several others, who afterwards appear'd in the Field against him. Nay the King himself, in his Letters to the King of *France* and to the Pope, affirms that Grant to have been made, " *de voluntate, concilio & con-" sensu, & ad procurationem Comitum, Ba-" ronum, & Procerum Regni, ipso Petro de " Gaveston hoc ignorante.* The Letters are dated, *apud Windshor* 16 *Juni Anno Reg.* 1. *ib. p.* 90. *Rymer's* 3 *Tom. Ann.* 1, 2, 3, 4, *Ed.* 2. is full of Papers relating to this *Peter de Gaveston.* By which it is manifest he was the greatest Favourite that ever Prince had (unless his Successors in Favour, the two *le Despensers* are to be excepted.) He by his pernicious Counsels led the King into such Measures and Difficulties, that the *Parliament* could not but take Notice of them, and *Anno* 5. *Reg. Ed.* 2. *Commissioners* were in full *Parliament* authorized under the great Seal to manage the Affairs of the Kingdom, and to put the King's Expences, and Method of Government, into to some Form and Regularity. These Commissioners were known by the Name of the *Ordeinors*, and by Reason that what they did was by Authority of Parliament, their Resolutions and Ordinances are entered upon the *Parliament-Roll*, among the rest of the Parliamentary Proceedings, and were in Fact observed as an Act of Parliament. And the *Sheriffs of Counties*, who were antiently elected in their Counties, came first to be nominated by the Chancellor, Treasurer, *&c.* by Vertue of an Article in their Ordinances. *sc.* " *Estre ceo* " *nous ordeinomus que Viscounts soient desor-* " *mes mis par le Chancelier & Tresorer &* " *les autres du Conseil qui serront present,* " *& si le Chancelier ne soit present, soit mis* " *par le Tresorer & Barons del Exchequer,* " &c. We farther Ordain, that for the fu- " ture, the Sheriffs be *put* in by the Chan- " cellor, Treasurer, and such others of the " Council, who shall be present; but if " the Chancellor shall not be present, let " them be put in by the Treasurer and " Barons of the Exchequer *, *&c.* Which is an Instance of the great Authority of these Ordeinors, since they could cause so considerable an Alteration in the *Common-*

* *Lord Chief Justice* Coke *refers this Alteration of the Law, to the Statute* 9 Ed. 2. *and takes no Notice of any of these Ordinances.*

Law;

Law; and this very Article was afterwards so much approved of, that it was 9 *Ed.* 2. turn'd into a formal *Statute*, and is printed in the Book. The Statute 12 *R.* 2. is in Substance the same with this Article, only there are more Officers mention'd, as of Necessity to be present at the Nomination, than there are either in the Article or the Statute of *Ed.* 2. *Vid. Coke* 2. *In. p.* 175.

Their *Ordinances* are very remarkable, and well worth reading from the Beginning to the End; but it would too much fill this Paper to transcribe the whole *Record*, and for that Reason I shall mention but one more Article besides what I directly quoted it for; and that is this, *Art.* 9. " *Pur ceo que le Roy ne doit emprendre fait* " *de Guerre contre nully, sans common Assent* " *de son Barnage, pur mults perils que pur-* " *ront avenir a luy, & a son Realme, Nous* " *ordeinomus, que le Roy desormes ne aile hors* " *de son Realme n'emprenge contre nully fait* " *de Guerre, sans common Assent de son Bar-* " *nage, & ceo in Parliament; Et si autre-* " *ment face & sur cela emprise face so-* " *mondre son Service, soit le Somon pur* " *nul*, &c. Whereas the King ought not to " undertake any Act of War against any " Person, without the common Assent of " his Baronage, by Reason of many Dan- " gers which may thereby happen to him-

" self

" ſelf and to his Realm; * *We therefore ordain*,
" That for the future the King do not go
" out of his Realm, nor undertake any Act
" of War againſt any Perſon without the
" common Aſſent of his Baronage, and
" that in Parliament. And if he ſhall Act
" otherwiſe, and upon any Enterprize
" which he ſhall have in View, ſhall cauſe
" thoſe who hold of him by any Service,
" (*viz.* Military) to be ſummoned to at-
" tend him, let ſuch Summons be null. I do not make any Reflections upon this ſurprizing Clauſe, but think it to be worth obſerving, that in this Clauſe the Ordeinors did not only inſtitute, that for the future the King ſhould not undertake any War without the Conſent of his Baronage, but they recite it as part of the Law *then already in being* (which it is not probable they would do in ſo publick a manner unleſs it was notoriouſly ſo) for the Clauſe begins, Whereas *the King ought not to undertake*, &c. *We therefore ordain*, &c. So that were thoſe Perſons, who now plead nothing elſe but the *Royal Prerogative* to juſtifie themſelves for having made the moſt pernicious *and deſtructive Peace* that ever Nation *ſuffered*, to be try'd before a *Parliament*, of Sentiments like to that of which we now ſpeak,

* Vid. *L' Stat.* 1 $\frac{2}{3}$ *W.* 3. *Ca.* 2. Section 3.

ſpeak, I believe it would not be a long Debate, whether they ſhould be puniſhed capitally or not.

The other Article which I intend to tranſcribe, belongs entirely to this *Peter de Gaveſton*, and contains all the Articles upon which he was condemn'd, together with the *Judgment of the Ordeinors* thereupon, *&c.*

If any Reader deſires to examine this Record, or any other to which I may refer, it may be of Service to him to let him know there is a tollerable fair Copy of the *Parliamentary Records* in the *Inner Temple Library*, which were left to the Society by the late learned Mr. *Petty*. It is a Copy that I think may be depended upon, becauſe at the end of the Volumes there is a *Convenit cum Recordo*, atteſted under the Hands of the Clerks who tranſcrib'd and examined them.

Rot. Parl. 5. E. 2.

" *Pur ceo que connue choſe* " *eſt, & par le Examinement* " *des Prelatz, Counts & Ba-* " *rons, Chivalers & autres bonns Gentz* " *du Royalme, trovez, Que* Pierre de Ga- " veſton, *ad mal-menez, & mal conſeillez no-* " *ſtre Seigneur le Roy, & l'a enticee a mal* " *faire en divers maneres & deceivances.* " *En accoillant a luy tout le treſor le Roy,* " *& l'ad eſloigne hors du Royalme. En at-* " *treant a luy Royal poer & Royal dignitee* " *comen allyance faire de Gentz par Sermens*

" *de*

" *de vivre & morir ovesque luy, encounter*
" *toutz gentz, & ceo par le tresor que ill*
" *purchase de jour en jour,* enseigneurant *sur*
" *l'Estate l'Roy & de la Coronne, en destructi-*
" *on du Roy & du People; & especialment*
" *enloignant le Coer le Seigneur de ses liges*
" *Gentz en despisant leurs Counseils. Nient*
" *soeffrant bones Ministers faire ley deterre,*
" *en ostant les bons Ministers mettant ceux de*
" *sa Coviegne, aux ibien aliens come autres,*
" *qui a sa volunte & a son comandement offen-*
" *dent droit & ley de terre. En parnant terres,*
" *tenements & Baillies du Roy a luy & a ses*
" *Heires. Et ad fait que le Roy ad done*
" *terres & tenements de sa Coronne as divers*
" *gentz, a grant damage & descrese de le*
" *State le Roy & de sa Coronne; & ceo ausi*
" *bien puis l'ordeignment que le Roy granta as*
" *Ordeinors de faire, au profit de ly & de son*
" *People, come devant; encounter l'ordeign-*
" *ment des Ordeinors. Et maintient Robbeours,*
" *Homicides,* &c. *& les fait avoir le Char-*
" *tre le Roy de pees, endonnant hardement a*
" *misfesours de pis-faire. Et menant le Roy,*
" *enterre de guerre sans common Assent de*
" *son Barnage, en peril de son Corps, & en*
" *destruction du Royalme, Et en fesaunt*
" *sealer blaunches chartres, de sous le grant*
" *Seale le Roy, en deceit & distreritance le*
" *Roy & de sa Coronne & encounter son ho-*
" *mage. Et feloneßement, fauxement &*
" *traiterousment ad fait les choses susdites, a*
" *grant*

" *grant dishonour & damage du Roy, &*
" *desheretison de la Coronne & a destru-*
" *ction du People en moltes Maneres,*
" *& ovesque ceo nous eant regard,* &c.
" Whereas it is notoriously known, and
" by the Inquiry of the Prelates, Earls,
" and Barons, Knights, and other good
" People of the Realm, it is found, *That*
" *Peter de Gaveston* has evilly advis'd and
" counsell'd our Lord the King, and has
" entic'd him to do Evil in divers Manners.
" *That* he cheated the King in his Trea-
" sure, and sent it beyond the Seas. *That*
" he encroached to himself Royal Power
" and Dignity, in making People engage
" themselves by Oaths to live and die with
" him against all Men; all which he effect-
" ed by Means of the Treasure which he
" daily procured, Lording it over the Estate
" of the *King, and of the Crown*, to the
" Destruction of the *King, and of his Peo-*
" *ple. That* he especially alienated the
" Heart of the Lord (*the King*) from his
" Lieges, and caused him to despise their
" Councils. *That* he did not suffer good
" Ministers to execute the Law of the Land,
" by displacing such good Ministers, and
" employing those of his own Confedera-
" cy, as well Aliens as others, who at his
" Will, and his Commandment, act con-
" trary to Right, and the Law of the Land.
" *That* he took Lands, Tenements, and

" Farms,

" Farms, from the King to himſelf, and " his Heirs (*i. e.* a Fee Simple.) *That* he " caus'd the King to grant Lands and Te- " nements of the Crown, to ſeveral Peo- " ple, to the great Damage and Decreaſe " of the Eſtate of the King and of his " Crown. And this he did as well ſince " the Ordinance which the King granted " to the Ordeinors to make for the Benefit " of *himſelf and his People*, as before, con- " trary to the ſaid Ordinance of the Ordein- " ors. *That* he ſupports Robbers, Mur- " therers, *&c.* procuring for them the " King's Charters of *Pardon*, by which he " encourages Evil-doers to do worſe. " That he carried the King into a Land " of War without the common Aſſent of " the Baronage, to the Peril of his Body, " and to the Deſtruction of the Realm. " *That* he cauſed the Great Seal to be put " to Blank Charters (*The Word ſeems here* " *to ſignify any Letters Patent, and is not* " *confin'd to any particular Senſe)* in De- " ceit and Diſinheritance of the King and " of his Crown, and againſt his Homage, " *feloniouſly*, *falſly* and *traiterouſly* he did " the Things before-mentioned, to the " Diſhonour and Damage of the King, " to the Diſheriſon of the Crown, and " Deſtruction of the People in many Man- " ners. To which we having Regard, " *&c.* And then they recite how that by

the Ordinance of King *Ed.* 1. he had abjur'd the Realm, and that the King himself (then being Prince) did at the same Time abjure the Company of the said *Peter de Gaveston* for ever. They farther recite, that since that Abjuration, " *Par cum-*
" *mun Assent de tout le Royaulme & du Roy*
" *& de ly meme Prelatz, Countees & Ba-*
" *rons*". That by the common Assent of
" the whole Realm, and of the King,
" and of the said Prelats, Earls, and Ba-
" rons, *&c.* he was for ever banish'd the Kingdom, and that his return into it was not by common Consent, but the Contrivance of particular Persons, to the great Prejudice of the People. " *Per qual eschuire*
" *nous ordeinomus, par Vertue de la Commissi-*
" *on nostre Seigneur a nous grant, que Piers*
" *de Gaveston, come appiert Ennemy le Roy*
" *& de son People*; to avoid which we
" ordain, by Vertue of the Commission
" of our Lord unto us granted, That *Peter*
" *de Gaveston*, as he appears an Enemy of
" the King and of his People, *&c.* be for
" ever banished out of all the King's Domi-
" nions, and if he shall ever return into the
" *Seigneury le Roy adunque soit fait de luy,*
" *come del Ennemy du Roy, du Royaulme &*
" *de son People*, Seignory of the King,
" then let it be done unto him, as unto the
" Enemy of the King, of the Kingdom,
" and of the People, *&c.*

These

These Articles are charged upon him for Treason. Yet it would be difficult for those People who are Friends to the late *Ministry*, consistent with the Principles they lay down, to prove any one of them to be such: So that if any Treason be in them, it must be *accumulative*. For what do these Articles amount to? Why, *First*, He gave bad Counsel to the King, and appropriated to himself a great Part of the *Royal Treasure*. I believe no Man who has been a *Treasurer*, will be willing to think this more than a *Breach of Trust*, a *Misdemeanour*, or something of that *Nature*. Tho' the *Crimen peculatûs* has something of a deeper Guilt in it now, when the Pillage is of Money given by the publick, and appropriated to particular Uses (which makes the Crown to be in Subsidies of this Nature only as it were a *Common Trustee*) than when the *Robbery* cou'd extend no farther than the cheating the King of the Rents and Profits of his *Demesnes*. 2. He procur'd People by a liberal Distribution of his Money, to engage themselves by Oaths to live and die with him. The People who have been so industrious in raising the late *Mobs*, to give such hearty *Declarations* in their Favour, cou'd they have *constru'd* this to be *Treason*. 3. He *alienated* the King's Heart from his Nobles, making him to despise their Counsels, and to turn out *good*

Miniſters, and to put in *bad ones* of his own *Confederacy*: This ſeems to want no *Application*. 4. He took Grants of Land from the King to himſelf, and his Heirs. It has been already ſhewn, that the Grant of the Earldom of *Cornwall*, was almoſt *Parliamentary*. 5. He procured Grants of Lands to ſeveral other Perſons, to the *Deſtruction of the Crown*. 6. He alſo procured Charters of Pardon to ſeveral *Murtherers*, *Robbers*, &c. to the emboldening of wicked Men. How! could this be *Treaſon* in *Gaveſton*, and not ſo in *Walter Reynolds*, *Biſhop of Worceſter*, who was then *Keeper of the Seal*, and upon whom it was incumbent, *ex Officio*, to ſee that nothing illegal ſhould paſs the Seals? and yet he was never call'd to Accompt, or queſtioned for theſe Things. Beſides, is not the King's Power of *pardoning Criminals* as clear a Branch of the *Prerogative*, as that of making *Peace and War*, or the creating a *Dozen of Peers* in the *midſt of a Seſſion*, in the *midſt of a Debate*. What then was his Crime? Why! it was certainly that *Abuſe* of the Royal Prerogative, which he adviſed the King to exerciſe. For when Mercy is ſo indiſcreetly uſed, as to give Encouragement to Offenders, by taking away the Fear of Puniſhment, it becomes a Grievance and Cruelty to the reſt of the World. And is not an *Attempt* to render one Branch

of

of the *Constitution useless*, as fatal an *Abuse* of the Prerogative, as the pardoning a few Criminals: For it is absurd to think, that *either House* can ever with Success, oppose it self to the Designs of a Court, if an *extempore Creation* of a Majority can be *justified.*

I shall not recapitulate any more of the Articles against him, but leave the Reader to make such Observations upon them as he thinks fit. Every one knows how the Affair of this *unhappy Earl* ended. He after his Exile ventur'd to return into *England* without the Permission of the Barons, trusting to the Protection of the King; which the Barons resenting, immediately took up Arms, and *forced both the King* and *Gaveston* to fly to the Castle of *Scarborough*, where the King left him, whilst he himself went to gather a Strength for his Relief: But the Barons took the Castle before it cou'd be reliev'd, and carry'd *Gaveston* to *Dadington*, where *Guy, Earl of Warwick*, ordered him to be beheaded, *tanqum legum Regni subversorem & publicum proditorem communi Judicio*, Vid. Thom. Walsing. Ypod. Neus: Int. Ang. & Norm p. 501. *ac etiam ejus*, Histor. p. 101.

It is remarkable in this Case, that the *Earl of Lancaster*, and several other Persons, who, as was before observed, were Witnesses to the Grant of the Earldom of

 Corn-

Cornwall, were the Chiefs of the Party who pursued him to his Death; and after his Death, they carried the Matter with so high a Hand, that *Anno* 1313. *Ed.* 2. 7. they obliged the King to consent to an Act of general Pardon to all those who had been concern'd in the Death of *Gaveston*, Rot. Par. 17 *E.* 2. p. 1. M. 14. So far was the King from being able to revenge it.

In *Rymers*'s *Fæd.* Tom. 3. p. 448. there is even the King's general Release to the Barons for all such Jewels, or other Moveables of his own, which they might have taken or destroyed in their pursuit of *Gaveston.*

The *Two Spencers* succeeded to *Gaveston* both in Favour and Insolence, and *Anno* 15 *Ed.* 2. they were condemned of High Treason by the *Lords in Parliament* (without the Consent of either *Prelates or Commons*) who only consented to the Act for their Banishment after the Judgment given. The Articles upon which they were condemned are very remarkable, but too long to be inserted in this Paper in the Original Language, The Substance of them, as near as I can collect them, is as follows.

Al Honour de Dieu, &c. 1. " *That Sir* " *Hugh*, the Son, drew a Writing, where- " by he endeavoured to engage Sir *John* " *Gifford*, and others, in a Conspiracy, to " force

" force the King to do whatsoever he wou'd " have him." To support this Accusation, there is in the Articles inserted the Copy of a Writing which I here litterally translate, that every Reader may for himself, judge how far it will justifie, and prove a Charge of High Treason.

" *Sc. Homage*, and the *Oath of Allegi-* " *ance*, are more by reason of the *Crown*, " than of the *Person* of the King; Which " appears, for that before the *Crown* de- " scends, there is no Allegiance due to the " *Person expectant*: Wherefore in Case " the King carries not himself by *Reason* " in Right of the *Crown*, his Leiges are " bound by *Oath made* to the Crown, to " *remove* the King, and the State of the " Crown *by Reason*, and otherwise the " Oath ought not to be observed. But it " may be ask'd, how the King in such a " Case is to be dealt with, *by Suit at Law*, " *or by Force* (*par Suite de ley ou per as-* " *pertee*) by Suit at Law a Man can have " no Redress, for he can have no Judge " but by the King. In which Case, if the " *King's Will* be not according to *Reason*, " nothing but Error wou'd be maintained " and confirmed; wherefore to *save their* " *Oath*, when the King will *not Redress* " what is injurious to the People, and pre- " judicial to the Crown, they ought to *pro-* " *ceed with Rigor*, for he is bound by

" *Oath to govern* his People, and his Leiges " are bound to *govern in aid of him*, and " in *default* of him.

2. " That by their evil Counsel they " caused the King never to grant his Pre- " sence (which he by Right ought to do " to his great Men) nor any Petitions but to " such Persons as they thought fit: Which " was contrary to the King's Duty and " Oath.

3. " That they will not suffer the Great " Men, *nor good Counsellors to approach the* " *King*, to give him Counsel, by which " they usurp'd to themselves *Royal Power* " *and Authority* over the Person of the " King, to the great Dishonour and Dan- " ger of the Realm.

4. " That in Order to attain their " wicked Purpose, and to the Disinheri- " tance of the Great Men, and Destruction " of the People, they put out good and a- " greeable Ministers who *were placed by* " *Assent*, and put in others false and wicked " of their own Party.

5. " They maliciously advised the *King* " *to raise Arms against his People* in *Glou-* " *cestershire*, contrary to the *Great Char-* " *ter*, and the Award of the Peers of the " Land.

6. " Whereas the Earl of *Hereford*, and " Lord *Wigmore*, were assign'd by the " King to make War upon *Lleuellin Bren*,

" who

" who ſurrendered himſelf to thoſe Lords
" at the King's Grace and Pleaſure. The
" ſaid Sir *Hugh*, Father and Son, accroach-
" ing to themſelves Royal Power and Au-
" thority, took the ſaid *Lleuellin* out of the
" Lords Hands, and carried him to their
" Caſtle of *Cardiff*, where pretending a Ju-
" riſdiction which they had not, they cau-
" ſed him to be hang'd, drawn, beheaded,
" and quarter'd.

7. " That they evilly adviſed the King
" to take into his Hands, the Lands of Sir
" *Hugh Audelye*, the Son, who was fore-
" judg'd without Proceſs, contrary to the
" Law of the Land.

8. " Whereas the King had granted by
" Letters Patents to the Earl of *Warwick*,
" in full Parliament, that after his Death
" his Executors ſhould have his Lands till
" his Heir was of full Age; they cauſed
" the King, without Cauſe, to repeal,
" and by their evil Counſel defeated what
" the King had granted in Parliament, to
" the Diſhonour of the King, and againſt
" Reaſon.

9. " That they would not ſuffer the King
" to take reaſonable Fines of the Peers, &c.
" when they entred upon their Fees, as
" had been uſed before that Time: Ma-
" king the *King to do againſt his Oath in*
" *Parliament*.

10. " That

10. " That by wicked Covetousness, " and *Royal Power*, they will not suffer " the King to hear, or do Right to the " Great Men, upon what they present un- " to him touching the disheriting the " Crown, and them, as to the Lands " which were *the Templars*. Also by *u- " surped Power Royal*, they govern'd the " King, his Council, and his Prelates, to " the Damage and Dishonour of the King, " the Peril of his Oath, and the Destructi- " on of his People.

11. " Also, that no Bishops, &c. Elect, " who ought to be received of the King " when duly elected, cou'd come near him, " or obtain any Favour from him, until " they had paid a Fine to the said Sir *Hugh*, " Father and Son; neither cou'd any one " else obtain any Favour from the King " without paying a Fine unto them. *Up- " on these Articles Judgment was given a- " gainst them in these Terms.*

" Which Wickednesses are notorious " and true, as it is found by the Exa- " mination of the Earls, Barons, and " other Peers of the Land: Wherefore " we Peers of the Land, Earls, and " Barons, in the Presence of our Lord " the King, do award, That *Hugh le " De Spencer*, both Father and Son, " shall be disherited for ever, as Dis-

" heritors

" heritors of the Crown, and Ene-
" mies to the King and his People;
" and be baniſhed the Kingdom of
" *England*, never to return again, un-
" leſs it be by the Aſſent of the King,
" and by the Aſſent of the Prelates,
" Earls, and Barons in Parliament
" duly Summon'd. And if they are
" found in *England* after that Day;
" (*ſc.*the Day appointed them for avoid-
" ing the Realm) or if they return'd
" after that Day, then to be done unto
" as unto the Enemies of the King
" and Kingdom.

N, B. This in the printed Copy is called *Exilium* Hugonis le De Spencer *patris & filii*, Old Stat. *per Berthelett*, 1540.

I ſhall not waſt the Reader's Time in making Obſervations upon theſe Articles: The ſame might be made almoſt, as upon thoſe againſt *Gaveſton*.

The *Spencers* maintain'd their Ground however, by Vertue of their Credit with the King (notwithſtanding the Judgment upon theſe Articles) about Four Years longer; for it was not till the 19° *Ed.* 2. that they were put to Death. The *Queen*, and *Prince Edward*, afterwards King *Edward* 3. in that Year came over from *France*, whether they had retired, and maintain'd a kind of War againſt *Ed.* 2. wherein they had the

better,

better, and purſued *Hugh Spencer, the Father*, to *Briſtol*, where he was taken and hang'd, drawn and quarter'd as a *Traytor*, if you will believe *Daniel*, without any Form of Law. *Spencer* the younger, who was taken Priſoner at the ſame Time, was arraigned for Treaſon before Juſtice *Truſſell* in a peculiar ſort of Form, which was by way of Speech made againſt him. The Subſtance of which, as I have been able to contract it, is as follows; *ſc.* " *Hugh le De*
" *Spencer, in the Parliament* held at *Weſt-*
" *minſter* in the 15th Year of the King that
" now is, your Father and you were ad-
" judged to be *Traytors*, and *Enemies to the*
" *Realm*, and were baniſhed as ſuch, ne-
" ver to return without the conſent of King
" and Parliament duly ſummon'd; contra-
" ry to which Award, your Father, and
" you, have been found in Court without
" Warranty. And you *Hugh*, as you re-
" turn'd into the Kingdom, did feloniouſly
" rob Two Merchant Ships (* *Droman-*
" *des*) to the Value of 40000 *l.* After
" this Felony you came to the King, and
" cauſed him to *take Arms againſt Peers* of
" the Realm, *&c.* contrary to the *Great*
" *Charter.* And alſo accroaching to your
" ſelf Royal Power, you and your Adhe-

* Q. de hoc Vocabulo.

" rents

" rents did feloniously rob the good Peo-
" ple of the Realm. And by means of *An-
" drew Harley*, and other Traytors, you
" murthered the good *Earl of Hereford*,
" and several other Persons at *Burrough-
" bridge*. And did there cause to be taken
" the most honourable Lord *Thomas*, *the
" good Earl of Lancaster*, whom by a *false
" Record against Law*, and the *Great Char-
" ter*, you caused to be murthered, martyr-
" ed, and put to Death. Also in the same
" Place you caused several other Barons and
" Knights to be hang'd, drawn and quar-
" ter'd, contrary to Law, and the Great
" Charter, in order to get their Estates.
" You also advised the King to an Expediti-
" on into *Scotland*, where he lost 20000
" Men, to the Dishonour and Damage of
" the Realm.

" *Hugh*, this Treason and Tyranny
" would not satisfie you, but by Royal
" Power gain'd over the King, you de-
" stroyed the Franchises of Holy Church,
" taking the Possessions of the Church to
" your own Use. And whereas you knew
" that God had wrought several Miracles
" by the good Earl of *Lancaster*, whom you
" had caused to be murthered, you placed
" Guards upon the Church where he was
" buried, that none might enter to Wor-
" ship God, and his Saints. You after this
" advised the King to grant Lands to the
" Earl

" Earl of *Winchester*, and several other
" Traytors, to the Disherison of the Crown.
" You also gave a great Sum of Money to
" your Adherents in *Guyenne*, where the
" Queen and her Son then were, to destroy
" them. *Hugh*, your Father, and your
" self, and several other Traytors, did by
" Force oblige several Persons to Swear,
" to Support and Maintain you in your
" Quarrels, *&c.* You at the same Time
" knowing such *Confederacies to be False*
" *and Traiterous.* And whereas you and
" the other Traytors knew that the Queen
" and Prince were arrived in the King-
" dom, you caused the King to withdraw
" himself out of the Kingdom; you feloni-
" ously taking with *you the Treasure* of the
" Realm, *contrary to the Great Charter.*
" *Hugh*, you are found to be a Traytor,
" wherefore all the good People of the
" Land by common Assent do Award, that
" you *are found as a Thief, and therefore*
" *shall be hang'd: As a Traytor, and there-*
" *fore shall be drawn and quarter'd.* And
" for that you have been *outlawed by the*
" *King and Parliament, you shall be behead-*
" *ed.* And for that you have *abetted, and*
" *created Disturbances between the King*
" *and Queen, and others of the Realm, you*
" *shall be embowelled, and your Bowels burn-*
" *ed.* Withdraw Traytor, Tyrant, and
" go take your Judgment, attainted, wic-
" ked

" ked Traytor." Upon this he was imme-diately executed, by Vertue of the *Act of Banishment and Attainder* which had passed against him; for when this Remarkable Speech was made against him, there was no Trial had either by Common Jury, or by Peers; he being then *Earl of Gloucester*. Vid. *Henricum de Knighton de event. Angl. infr. Scrip.* 10 Co. 2547. The Barons in both these Disputes got the better of the Royal Favourites, but yet it cost several of the most considerable of them their Lives; among whom, the chief Man was *Thomas Earl of Lancaster*, whom 15 *Regni Ed.* 2. the King got into his Power, and beheaded at *Pomfrett Castle*. The whole Record of the King's Proceedings against him is printed in *Rymer*'s 3d *Tom. p.* 936. and very well deserves to be read by Persons who are Curious in Things of this Nature.

However fatal these Disputes were to the Barons concern'd in them, yet their Country did afterwards sufficiently testifie their Approbation of all their Proceedings; for that Judgment against the *Earl of Lancaster*, was in the succeeding Reign revers'd *as illegal*; and the common People express'd so great a Veneration for him (that according to the Humour of the Age) they believed Variety of Miracles which were reported of him, and *Anno* 1389 he was *canonized for a Saint*; upon much *better Reasons* than any had been for *some Hundreds of Years* before him, since he died a *Martyr* to the *Liberty of his Country.*

4 *Ed.* 3. *Roger Mortimer* was by the Lords, *&c.* in Parliament, *attainted* of Treason, and executed. The Rolls upon which his particular Treasons, Felonies, *&c.* are entred, is (as Mr. *Prynn* informs us) so mouldred, that a great part of it cannot be read, for which Reason the following Articles against him are transcribed out of *Henry de Knighton, de Even. Angl. Coll.* 2556. *infra Scrip. decem.*

1. " Primieriement. *Que par la ove or-*
" *deine fuist al Parlement de* Londres *pro-*
" *chein a pres le Coronnement le Roy, Que*
" *quatres Evesques, quatres Contes, &* 6
" *Barons dussent estre pres du Roy, pour le*
" *Counseller issint que toutz fois* 4 *y fuissent.*
" *Cest a Savoir, un Evesque, un Conte, &*
" *dieux Barons, a Moynez, & que nulle grosse*
" *besoigne soit fait sans leur Assent, & que*
" *Chescune respondist dez cez fetz pur son*
" *temps; le dit* Roger *nient eyant regard al*
" *dit Assent,* accrocha a ly Royal Povere,
" *& le Government del Realme sur le Estate*
" *le Roy ousta & fist oustre & mettre Mini-*
" *stres en l' oustele le Roy & aillours par my*
" *le Realme a ce volunte de ceux que fuerunt*
" *de son accorde. Et myst* Jean Wyardet *&*
" *altres entour le Roy despier ses faits & ses*
" *ditz. Issint que le Roy fuist entyele manere*

" *envy-*

" *envyronne de ces Ennemys qil poet riens fairé*
" *de sa volunte mes auxi come un Homme de*
" *South altre Garde.*

2. " *Par la ou le Piere nostre Seigniour le*
" *Roy feust a* Kenilworth *par ordeinances des*
" *Pieres de la terre, a dimorer illonques a ses*
" *eses, pur estre Servi come afferreit uni tiele*
" *Seigneur, Le dit* Roger *par reall povare*
" *a ley accroche, nelessa tant quil l'eust devers*
" *luy a sa volunte. Et ordyna quil fuist*
" *fauxement traiterousement & felonissement*
" *mordre & tue.*

3. " *Ensy le dit* Roger *fist defendre par*
" *briefe le Roy sous le grant Seale que null*
" *vensist al Parlyment de Salusbury, a force*
" *& Armes sour quan qil poet forfere devers*
" *le Roy. Et la vynt le dit* Roger *& altres*
" *de sa Covygne al force & Armes al dit Par-*
" *lyment contre la dyte defence, par quoy plu-*
" *sours de la terre come le Conte de* Lanca-
" stre *& altres Sachans la manere de sa ve-*
" *nue ne vyndrent point. Et come par la ou*
" *les Prelats estoint Assemblez al dit Parly-*
" *ment, en un Meason pur Counseiller sur les*
" *besoignez le Roy & de Realme; le dit* Roger
" *debrusa les eos de la Measone ovez gentz des*
" *Armez sour les ditez Prelats, & les manas-*
" *sa de vye & de membre sils fuissent si hardys*
" *a dire ove faire riene en contre sa volunte*
" *& ordynances, E en meme le Parlyment fist*
" *tant que le Roy luy fist Conte de la* Marche

 " &

" *& luy dona plusours terres & tenementz* " *en Disherison de la Coronne.* *E puis mena* " *le dit* Roger *& ceux de sa Covygne nostre* " *Seigneur le Roy, Armez sur le conte de* " Lancastre *& altres Pieres de la terre tan-* " *que a* Winchester *la ove yls estoient venan-* " *cez devers le Roy au dit Parlyment de* Sa-" lusbury. *Par quoy le dit Conte & les al-* " *tres piers de la terre per eschewer le peril que* " *poet avenir, a la Reverence le Roy depar-* " *tirent & aylerent en vers lour pays dolons* " *qils ne point ove lour Seigneur Lege parlere* " *ne Conseillere come ils deveront.*

4. " *Ensi le dit* Roger *fist le Roy Chiva-* " *cher forciblement sur le Conte de* Lanca-" stre *& altres Pieres de Realme que estoint* " *ordeinez devoir estre pres du Roy pur luy* " *Conseiller. Et entant les Enchassa par force* " *que le dit Conte & altres Grantz del* " *Realme que voilerent profit au Roy, se* " *mistrent a la Grace le Roy, sauve erous* " *vye & Membre & qils ne fussent Desherits ne* " *altrop grant ranson, Mestils furent my au* " *trop grant rauson, que lours terre vendront* " *a tou jours. Et les altres fist enchaser de* " *la terre a Seizer lours terres* contre la " fourme de la grant Chartre & Ley de " terre.

5. " *Ensy par la ove le dit* Roger *savoit* " *biene qe le Piere nostre Seigneur le Roy* " *estoit morte enterne, il par altrez de sa Co-*

" *vygne*

" *vygne en desceivance manere, fist entendre*
" *al* Edmund *Conte de* Kent, *qil fuist envie,*
" *par quoy le dit Conte fuist moult desirous de*
" *savoir le verite,* E *fist espier par totez les bo-*
" *nez voiez que savoit, tanke le dit* Roger
" *par reall power aluy accroche fist prendre al*
" *Parlyment de* Winchester *le dit Conte de*
" Kent, *e procura qil fuist illo neques mys*
" *a la mort.*

6. " *Ensy le dit* Roger *fist le Roy doner*
" *a luy ses enfantz ea ses alies Chastieles, Vil-*
" *les, Maneres & Franchises en* Engliterre,
" Ireland, *& Gales en descresse de sa Co-*
" *ronne.*

7. " *Ensy le dit* Roger *en desceivance ma-*
" *nere fist les Chivalers des Contez, al dit*
" *Parlyment al Roy de chescune ville de* En-
" gliterre, *que respond par quatre, & le pro-*
" *vost en Eyre un Homme de Armes a lour*
" *costages en sa Guerre de* Gascoigne *par un*
" *An: la quele charge le dit* Roger *avoit*
" *compasse a tourner ceol avoir en altre profit*
" *pur luy & altres de sa Covygne en destruction*
" *de People.*

8. " *Ensy le dit* Roger *par real povare a*
" *luy accroche fist mander letters suth le grant*
" *Chartre, au plusours grants Chivalers &*
" *altres qe ils venesent al Roy qeu part qil*
" *fuist & a lour venue le fist chargere qils se ad-*
" *dressent daler en* Gascoigne *ou qils feissent*
" *fyn oue ranson a sa volunte: Des queus as-*

" *cunez fierent fyn grevous & tout le pluis est*
" *venuz en profit le dit* Roger.

9. " *Ensy le dit* Roger *faustment & mali-*
" *ciousment fist le discorde enter le Piere no-*
" *stre Seigneur le Roy & la Rayne sa Com-*
" *paigne & la fist entendre qe si ele out venuz*
" *a luy qil le out tue de cotele, ove altre arme*
" *ove altre manere de mordre & par tieles*
" *cause, & altres sottilettes si fist il tant qe la*
" *Reine ne vynt pas devers son Seigniour al*
" *grant Dishonour du Roy & de tote le Realme*
" *& Damage par cas entemps avenir. Qe Dieu*
" *defende.*

10. " *Ensy le dit* Roger *sy ad pris &*
" *fait prendre divers luy & les altres de sa*
" *Compaigne de Tresor le Roy a sa volunte*
" *sanz nombre en denirs & Juagais en destru-*
" *ction du Roy. Issint qe le Roy nad drien de*
" *paiyer pur son vivre.*

11. " *Ensy le dit* Roger *sy ad fait prendre*
" *devers luy & devers ses aliez* 20 *Mille marz*
" *queux sont venuz* horz dez scozce pur la
" fourme de la pees *& rien est venu al profit*
" *du Roy.*

12. " *Ensy le dit* Roger *ces prizes par my*
" *le Realme auxi come Roy & Seigniour de*
" *tutte & entre luy & les altres de sa covygne*
" *merent al double des gentz & chivalez en la*
" *Compaigne le Roy, qe le Roy ne fist en de-*
" *struction del People sans fair payment altre*
" *que a leur volunte.*

13. " *Ensy*

13. " *Ensy le dit* Roger *parson real povare* " *fist le granter a la montance* 200 *Chivelerz* " *a ceoux d'* Ireland *qe avoint tuez les grantz,* " *&* *altres de la terre qe furent de la foye le* " *Roy encelles parties. Par la ove le Roy de* " *voit pluis test par reson, avoire vengee* " *lour mort qe pardonnez contre fourme de* " *Parlyment.*

14. " *Ensi le dit* Roger *compassa devoire* " *destrut les Noryes le Roy & les Secrettez le* " *Roy de quex il sy pluis affya, & susmyt al* " *Roy en Presence la Reigne, sa miere & des* " Eveskus *de* Nicole *& de* Salusberrie, *&* " *altris de Counseil de Roy qe les avant ditz* " *Secrettez le Roy, luy exciterent destre la* " *Covygne des Enemys par de la en destruccon* " *de sa miere & de lavant dit* Roger. *La* " *quele chose il afferma tant sour le Roy qe la* " *parole le Roy ne poet estre creu. Et cela* " *venderdi la nute gils estoint prizes a la myt* " *nuyt suant donke pur les Causes suse scriptes* " *& molt dezaltres chosez qe ne sont ore adyre* " *si fist le dit Roy prendre en la manere par* " *eide & avisement des privez & nurriez.*

Imprimis. " Whereas at the Parliament " held at *London*, immediately after the " King's Coronation, it was ordained, that " four Bishops, four Earls, and six Barons, " should be always near the King for his " Council; that is to say, one Bishop, one Earl, " and two Barons at the least, at once; and

 " that

" that no Affair of Consequence should be " transacted without their Consent; and " that each of them shou'd be responsible " for what was done during the Time of " their Attendance: The said *Roger* not ha- " ving regard to the said Assent, accroach'd " to himself Royal Power, and the Govern- " ment of the Realm, *above the Estate of the* " *King*; and put out the Ministers of the " Houshold of the King, and others in the " Realm, and he put in others at his own " Pleasure, such as were of his own Party. " And he plac'd *John Wyard*, and others a- " bout the King, to espy his Actions and " Words, so that the King was environ'd " in such manner by his Enemies, that he " could do nothing of himself, but was " like a Man in Ward.

2. " Also, whereas the King's Father " was at *Kenilworth* by Ordinance of the " Peers of the Land, to live there at his " Ease, and to be serv'd in a Manner fitting " for such a Lord, the said *Roger* by Ac- " croachment of Royal Power, did not rest " till he had him as it were a Prisoner at " will; and then he order'd him to be " carry'd to the Castle of *Berkeley*, where, " by him, or by those whom he plac'd a- " bout him, he was falsly, traiterously, and " feloniously murther'd and kill'd.

3. " Al-

3. " Alſo the ſaid *Roger* forbad by the
" King's Writ, under the Great Seal, that
" none ſhould come to the Parliament at
" *Salisbury* with Force and Arms, upon pain
" of forfeiting whatſoever they cou'd forfeit
" to the King; yet the ſaid *Roger*, and o-
" thers of his Party, came with Force and
" Arms to the ſaid Parliament, contrary to
" the ſaid Prohibition; for which Reaſon,
" ſeveral *Peers* of the Land, as the Earl of
" *Lancaſter*, and others, underſtanding the
" manner of his coming, did not come.
" And whereas at the ſaid Parliament, the
" Prelates were aſſembled *in one House* to
" conſult of the Affairs of the King, and of
" the Realm, the ſaid *Roger* with armed
" Men, broke open the Doors of the ſaid
" Houſe upon the Prelates, and threatned
" them of Life and Member, if they were
" ſo hardy as to do any Thing againſt his
" Will and Ordinance. And in the ſaid
" Parliament, the ſaid *Roger* caus'd the
" King to create him Earl of *March*, and
" to grant him ſeveral Lands and Tene-
" ments, to the Diſheriſon of the Crown.
" And afterwards the ſaid *Roger*, and thoſe
" of his Party, led the King armed as far as
" *Wincheſter*, againſt the Earl of *Lancaſter*,
" and other Peers of the Land, who were
" come thither in their Way to meet the
" King at his Parliament at *Salisbury*; for

" which Reaſon the ſaid Earl, and the o-
" ther Peers of the Land, to avoid the
" Miſchief that might have happened,
" out of Reſpect to the King, departed, and
" went to their own Countries, grieving
" that they might not ſpeak with, nor ad-
" viſe their Leige Lord as they ought.

4. " Alſo the ſaid *Roger* cauſed the King
" to March forcibly againſt the Earl of
" *Lancaſter*, and the other Peers of the
" Land who were appointed to be with
" the King to adviſe him And he pro-
" ſecuted them with ſuch Force, that the
" ſaid Earl, and the other Great Men of
" the Land, who wiſhed well to the King,
" ſubmitted to the King's Mercy, ſaving
" to themſelves Life and Member; and
" that they might not be diſinherited, nor
" have too great a Fine ſet upon them; yet
" he cauſed them to be fin'd ſo grie-
" vouſly, that if their Land was ſold right
" out, it wou'd but pay it. And the o-
" thers he caus'd to be driven out of the
" Nation, and their Lands to be ſeiz'd;
" *againſt the Form of the Great Charter, and*
" *the Law of the Land.*

5. " Whereas the ſaid *Roger* knew well,
" that the King's Father was dead and bu-
" ried, he by others of his Party, in de-
" ceitful manner, informed the Earl of *Kent*
" that he was alive: Wherefore the ſaid
" Earl

" Earl being desirous to know whether it " was so or not, used all the good Ways he " could to discover the Truth: Insomuch " that the said *Roger*, by his usurped Royal " Power, caused him to be apprehended " at the Parliament held at *Winchester*, and " so pursu'd him, that in that Parliament " he was put to Death.

" 6. Also the said *Roger* caus'd the King " to give to him and his Children, and his " Confederates, Castles, Towns, Manors " and Franchises, in *England*, *Ireland*, and " *Wales*, to the Decrease of the Crown.

7. " Also the said *Roger*, in deceitful man- " ner, made the Knights of Shires, at the said " Parliament, grant to the King one Man " at Arms of every Town in *England*, that " answered in Eyre, by four, and the Pro- " vost, at their Cost, for a Year, in his " Wars in *Gascoigne*: Which Charge he " contriv'd to turn it to the Profit of him- " self and Party, in Destruction of the " People.

" 8. Also the said *Roger*, by his said ac- " croached Royal Power, caused Summons " to be sent to many Great Knights and " others, under the Great Seal, that they " shou'd come to the King where-ever he " was, and when they came, he caus'd " them to be charg'd to prepare themselves " to go into *Gascoigne*, or to fine at his

" Plea-

" Pleasure: Which Fines were for the Benefit of him and his Party.

" 9. Also the said *Roger* falsely and maliciously caus'd Discord between the Father of our Lord the King, and the Queen his Wife, and possessed her, that if she went to him, she shou'd be kill'd with a Dagger, or otherwise murthered: And by this means, and his other Subtleties, he so order'd it, that she would not come near her Lord, to the great Dishonour of the King, and in time to come perhaps to the Mischief of the whole Realm. Which God forbid.

" 10. Also the said *Roger* had caused to be taken for himself and Party, as much of the King's Treasure as he pleas'd, without Tale, in Money and Jewels, to the Destruction of the King; insomuch that the King had not wherewithal to pay for his Victuals.

" 11. Also the said *Roger* caused to be taken for himself and Confederates, the 20000 Marks, which came out of *Scotland* for the Articles of Peace, without any Part of it coming to the Profit of the King.

" 12. Also the said *Roger* received the King's Duties and Purveyances throughout the Kingdom, as if he had been King; and he and his Party had with them

" double

" double the Company of Men and Horſe " that were with the King, to the De- " ſtruction of the People, they not paying " for their Quarters more than they " pleas'd.

" 13. Alſo the ſaid *Roger*, by his ſaid " uſurped Royal Power cauſed the King " to grant to the Mounting 200 *Iriſh*, of " thoſe who kill'd the Great Men and o- " thers, who were in the King's Faith in " thoſe Parts: Whereas the King ought " immediately to have reveng'd their Death, " rather than have pardoned them contrary " to the Statute and Aſſent of Parliament.

" 14. Alſo the ſaid *Roger* contriv'd to " have deſtroy'd the King's ſecret Friends, " in whom he had the moſt Confidence. " And he ſurmis'd to the King, in the Pre- " ſence of the Queen his Mother, the Bi- " ſhops of *Lincoln* and *Saliſbury*, and others " of the Council, that his ſaid ſecret Friends " had excited him to combine with his Ene- " mies beyond Sea, to the Deſtruction of " the Queen his Mother, and him the ſaid " *Roger*: And this he affirm'd ſo impudent- " ly upon the King, that the King cou'd " not be believ'd againſt what he had ſaid. " And for theſe things, and many others " not as yet fit to be declared, was he ap- " prehended, &c.

It

It is visible, that the greatest Point of Treason against *Mortimer*, was his being accessory to the Murther of the *King's Father*, *Edw.* II. after he was deprived of his Royal Dignity, and thereby reduced to the Condition of a private Man, and *in Fact a Subject to his Son*; which is not now, I believe, *suspected to be Treason* within the Statute. However it must be acknowledged, that this Judgment against *Mortimer* was afterwards revers'd. In the Parliament 28 *Ed.* 3. *n.* 7, to 14. *Roger Mortimer*, Cousin and Heir to this executed *Roger*, required by Petition, that this Judgment and Attainder pass'd 4 *Ed.* 3. *n.* 1. might be reviewed and examined, and for manifest Errors therein reversed. The only Error assigned upon this Petition, was, for that the Judgment was defective and erroneous, in that the said Earl was put to death and disinherited *sans nulle accusament, & sans este mesne au Jugement, au en respons*; that is, in short, without the Formalities of a Trial. For this Cause only, and not for any Error assigned as to the Substance of the Charge, was the Judgment reversed and set aside. So that it rather affirms than otherwise all the Points alledged in the Charge to be treasonable; for certainly it would have been more honourable for young *Roger* to have prov'd his

Uncle

Uncle not a Traytor, than to reſtore himſelf in Blood by an Error in point of Form.

In the ſame Parliament, 4 *Ed.* 3. the King charg'd the Earls and other Peers to give Judgment againſt *Simon de Beresford*, *Thomas Gurney*, *&c.* for being aiding and aſſiſting to the ſaid *Roger Mortimer* in his Treaſons and Felonies, *&c.* which *they ſcrupled to do, the ſaid* Simon *not being their Peer:* But at laſt, it appearing manifeſtly that they were concern'd in the ſaid Treaſons and Murther of *Ed.* 2. *(& Deſtruction du ſang Royal)* they as *Peers and Judges of Parliament*, did give Judgment of Death againſt them.

The Lord *Berkley*, in whoſe Caſtle *E.* 2. was murthered, was arraigned for the ſame Crime, who, for what Reaſon I cannot imagine, *wav'd his Peerage*, and put himſelf on the Trial of his Country, and was actually tryed for Treaſon before the King *by a Jury of Knights* in full Parliament, and by them acquitted. This Caſe being very remarkable, I think the whole Record deſerves to be printed.

" *Thomas de Berkele Miles venit coram Do-*
" *mino Rege in pleno Parliamento ſuo prædicto,*
" *& allocutus eſt hoc: Quòd cùm Dominus*
" *Edvardus, nuper Rex Angliæ, pater Domi-*
" *ni Regis nunc, in cuſtodiam ipſius Thomæ*
&

" *& ejusdem Johannis Mantravors, nuper ex-*
" *titit collatus, ad salvò custodiend. in castro*
" *ipsius Thomæ apud Berkele in comitatu Gla-*
" *vorum, & in eodem castro, in custodia ip-*
" *sorum Thomæ & Johannis murdratus extitit*
" *& interfectus; qualiter se velit de morte ip-*
" *sius Regis acquietare. Dicit quòd nunquam*
" *fuit consentiens, auxilians, seu procurans*
" *ad mortem suam, nec unquam scivit de morte*
" *suâ, usquam in præsenti Parliamento isto;*
" *& de hoc paratus est acquietare se, prout*
" *curia Regis consideraverit. Et super hoc*
" *quæsitus est ab eo, Ex quo? ipse est Domi-*
" *nus castri prædicti; & idem Dominus Rex*
" *in custodiam ipsorum Thomæ & Johannis*
" *extitit liberatus ad salvò custod. & ipsi*
" *custodiam ipsius Regis receperunt & accep-*
" *taverunt; qualiter se excusare possit, quin*
" *de morte ipsius Regis respondere debeat?*
" *Et prædictus Thomas dicit, quòd verum est,*
" *quòd ipse sit Dominus castri prædicti, &*
" *quòd ipse simul cum Johanne Mantravors*
" *custodiam ipsius Regis recepit, ad salvò*
" *custod. ut prædictum est; sed dicit, quòd eo*
" *tempore quo dicitur ipsum Dominum Regem*
" *esse murdratum & interfectum, fuit ipse*
" *taliter tantâ infirmitate apud Bradelye extra*
" *castrum prædictum detentus, quòd ei curre-*
" *bat memoriæ. Et super hoc dictum est ei,*
" *quòd ex quo cognovit quòd ipse simul cum*
" *dicto Johanne custodiam ipsius Domini Regis*

" *obtinuit,*

" *obtinuit, ut prædictum est, & ipse custodem*
" *& ministrum sub se posuit, ad custodiam de*
" *eo faciendam, si per aliquam infirmitatem*
" *excusari possit, quin respondere debet in hac*
" *parte? Et prædictus Thomas dicit, quòd*
" *ipse posuit sub se tales custodes & ministros*
" *in castro prædicto pro custodiâ faciendâ, à*
" *quibus ipse se confidebat ut de seipso, qui*
" *custodiam ipsius Regis simul cum prædicto*
" *Johanne Mantravors inde habuerunt; unde*
" *dicit quòd ipse de morte ipsius Domini Regis,*
" *auxilio, assensu, seu procuratione mortis suæ,*
" *in nullo est inde culpabilis.* Et de hoc
" de bono & malo ponit se super patriam.
" *Ideo venerunt inde juratores coram Domino*
" *Rege in Parliamento suo apud Westmonaste-*
" *rium, in Octabis sancti Hilarii proximè*
" *futuris, &c. Ad quam diem venit præ-*
" *dictus Thomas coram Domino Rege in pleno*
" *Parliamento, ac sil. Jurat. sc. Johannes*
" *Darci, &c. omnes milites, qui dic. super*
" *sacramentum suum, quòd prædictus Thomas*
" *de Berkele in nullo est culpabilis, prædicti*
" *Domini Edvardi Regis, patris Domini Re-*
" *gis nunc, nec de assensu, auxilio, seu procu-*
" *ratione mortis ejusdem: Et dicunt quòd tem-*
" *pore mortis ejusdem Dom. Edvardi Regis Pa-*
" *tris Dom. Regis, fuit ipse tali infirmitate gra-*
" *vatus, apud Bradeley extra castrum suum præ-*
" *dictum, quòd de vitâ ipsâ desperabat'. Ideo*
" *idem Thomas inde quiet. Et Jurat. quæsit.*

" *si*

" *si idem Thomas unquam subtraxit se occasione* " *prædictâ ? Dic. quòd non. Et quia idem* " *Thomas posuit custodem & ministrum sub se,* " *sc. Thomam de Gurney & Willielmum de* " *Ocle, ad custodiam de ipso Domino Rege fa-* " *ciendam, per quod idem Dominus Rex exti-* " *tit murdratus & interfectus, dat. est ei dies* " *coram Domino Rege nunc in proximo Par-* " *liamento suo, ad audiendum judicium suum,* " *&c. Et prædictus Thomas de Berkele inte-* " *rim committitur Radulpho de Nevill, Ma-* " *reschallo Hospitii Domini Regis, &c.*

In this *Parliament* they did not only think it Treason to kill the *King's Father*, but their Notion of it was so large, that Judgment of Treason was given against Sir *John Mantravers*, *Bogo de Bayons*, and *John de Veroil*, for being guilty of the Murther of *Edmund* Earl of *Kent*, who was no more than Uncle to the King:

Sir *William Thorpe*, one of the *Justices* of the *King's Bench*, and *Justice of Assize* in *Com. Lincoln.* 23 *Ed.* 3. against his Oath, took several Bribes from several People to stay an Exigent upon an Indictment for Felony, that shou'd have issued against them: For which he was try'd and convicted before the Earls of *Arundel*, *Warwick*, &c. to whom the King by a special Commission had referred the Examination of the Business.

Business. "*Ideo consideratum est per dictos*
"*Justitiarios assignatos ad judicandum se-*
"*cundum voluntatem Regis, & secundum*
"*Regale posse suum: Quòd quia prædictus*
"*Willielmus Thorpe, qui* sacramentum Do-
"mini Regis, quod erga populum suum
"habuit custodiendum, fregit malitiosè,
"falsè & rebelliter, *in quantum in ipso fuit,*
"*& ex causis supra dictis ipsum Willielmum*
"*expressè cognitis; Ideo suspendatur, &*
"*quòd omnia terræ & tenementa, bona &*
"*catalla sua remaneant forisfacta.*

The King by Writ stay'd the Execution, and in the Parliament 25 *Ed.* 3. *n.* 10. the Record of this Judgment was brought into the House of Lords, to have their Advice and Opinion concerning it, whether it was legal or not; and all the Lords, *nemine contradicente*, affirmed the Judgment to be good and legal. And it was thereupon agreed by *all the Lords*, that whenever the like Case shou'd happen, the King employing such of the Nobility as he should think proper, might do therein according to his own Pleasure: Under this Proviso however, that the said Judgment shou'd not be drawn into Precedent against any other Officers who shou'd break their Oaths, *but only against the Judges, who have the Laws of* England *in their Custody:* "*Contra eos tantum, qui prædictum sacra-*

" *mentum fecerunt* (Justitiariorum) *& fre-*
" *gerunt, & habent leges Angliæ regales ad*
" *custodiendum.*

The Precedents which have been hitherto cited are altogether Parliamentary, and I think it may be fairly concluded from them, that any Crime which had the Publick, as such, for its Object, and which cou'd properly be stiled, *an horrible Offence against the Safety of either King or Kingdom*, was constantly in Parliament adjudged to be *Treason*.

This therefore being the true Notion of High Treason at the *Common Law*; the next thing to be considered is, what Alteration or Change it may have undergone by reason of the Statute 25 *Ed.* 3. or any other. To which end I here transcribe it.

Item, " Whereas divers Opinions have
" been before this Time, in what Case
" Treason shall be said, and in what not:
" The King, at the request of the Lords,
" and of the Commons, hath made a De-
" claration in manner as hereafter follow-
" eth; (that is to say) when a Man doth
" compass or imagine the Death of our
" Lord the King, or of our Lady his Queen,
" or of their eldest Son and Heir; or if a
" Man doth violate the King's Companion,
" or the King's eldest Daughter unmarried,
" or

" or the Wife of the King's eldest Son and " Heir, or if a Man doth levy War against " our Lord the King in his Realm, or be " adherent to the King's Enemies in his " Realm, giving to them Aid and Comfort " in his Realm or elsewhere, and thereof " be probably attainted of open Deed by " the People of their Condition. And if a " Man counterfeit the King's Great or Pri- " vy Seal, or his Money. And if a Man " bring false Money into this Realm, coun- " terfeit to the Money of *England*, as the " Money called *Lushburgh*, or other like to " the said Money of *England*, knowing " the Money to be false, to merchandize or " make Payment in Deceit of our said Lord " the King, and of his People. And if a " Man slay the Chancellor, Treasurer, or " the King's Justices of the one Bench or the " other; Justices in Eyre or Justices of Assize, " and all other Justices assigned to hear and " determine, being in their Places doing " their Offices: And it is to be understood, " that in the Cases above rehearsed, that " ought to be judged Treason which ex- " tends to our Lord the King and his Royal " Majesty; and of such Treason the For- " feiture of the Escheats pertaineth to our " Lord, as well of the Lands and Tene- " ments holden of others as of himself. And " because that *many other like Cases of Trea-*

" *ſon* may happen in Time to come, which
" a Man cannot think nor declare at this
" preſent Time, it is accorded, That if a-
" ny other Caſe, ſuppoſed Treaſon, which
" is not above ſpecify'd, doth happen be-
" fore any Juſtices, the Juſtices ſhall tarry
" without any going to Judgment of the
" Treaſon, till the Cauſe be ſhewed *before*
" *the King and his Parliament*, whether it
" ought to be judged Treaſon or other Fe-
" lony.

This Act of Parliament was intended to be a ſtrong Bulwark for the Liberties of the People, againſt any Oppreſſions they might be liable to from the Crown. But now by a ſtrange kind of *Revolution*, it is made Uſe of by ſome to protect Miniſters againſt the juſt Reſentment and Proſecution of Parliament: *And an Act of Parliament is pleaded, in Barr to the Power of Parliaments.* But if we examine what the true Reaſon of making this Statute was, I believe it will be found to be no Ways favourable to their Cauſe. It has been already hinted, that before this Statute was made, the Adjudication of thoſe particular Actions which ſhould be puniſhed as Treaſonable, was altogether in the Cognizance of the ordinary Courts of Juſtice, and for Want of fixed Rules, almoſt diſcretionary in the Judges, and they being

being absolutely in the Power of the Crown, the Preservation of their Places inspired them with a wonderful Zeal to punish all such Crimes as Treason, which particularly affected the Prince, *as distinct from the Publick*. And then there was a very weighty Reason to induce the Prince, to desire the Doctrine of Treason to be as extensive, and also as ambiguous as possible; a considerable Revenue arose from it, for in High Treason, at the *Common Law*, all the Lands, *&c.* of the Criminal, from whatsoever Lord they were holden, were forfeited to the Crown; when as in other Cases the Lands, *&c.* escheated to the several Lords from whom they were held: And it is not improbable, but that the Judges, to improve their Interest at Court, did very often adjudge Cases to be Treason (which they ought not in strict Justice to have done) in order to secure a considerable Forfeiture to the Crown, *satisfying their Consciences* with this Consideration, that if a Man must be hang'd, it matter'd not much, whether it was for Treason or Felony; by which means the inferior Lords were dextrously cheated of the Benefit of their Escheats. This (as it really was a great Grievance) was complain'd of in Parliament about four Year before this Act was made. For *Rot. Parl.* 21 *Ed.* 3. the Commons petition, *That whereas some Justices* had lately adjudged Matters before them, to be *Treason and Accroachment of Royal Power*, whereby the Lords lost the Benefit of the Forfeiture of their Escheats, they desire that those Matters might be settled in certain.

The Answer to their Petition was not such as they expected, but they were forced to stay till 25° *Ed.* 3. This gives one a tolerable Idea of what our Ancestors intended by this famous Statute of Treasons. For certainly nothing can so well direct us to the Intention of Legislators, as the perfect Knowledge of the Mischief they intended to remedy and prevent. But let us quote a few Instances of those Treasons which were then look'd upon and esteem'd to be so great a Grievance. *Tr.* 21 *Ed.* 3 *pl.* 24. a Person was condemned and executed for Treason, for killing a Man who was riding to the King, to serve him in his Wars. *L.* 1. *Ass.* 22 *Ed.* 3. *pl.* 49. It was adjudged High Treason to kill a Man who was sent on an Errand from the King. But *Britton* goes much farther, for *p.* 43. He in the Person of the King, says, that it is, *Haute Trehison —— pur giser avec les Norrices de nos Enfants.* What Implications and Innuendoes must there be to make these Facts Treasons? How hard and unjust would it now be thought, was any Man to be hang'd, &c. only for lying *with the Court-Nurse?*

But

But these are not the only Reasons to induce one to think, that the Parliament in the making of this Statute, only intended to regulate the Jurisdiction of the inferior Courts of Justice. It may be shown from a much higher Authority, that what they did was wholly founded upon, and levelled against these Corruptions and Irregularities of the Judges. *The Petition of the Commons* upon which this Act of Parliament was drawn, sufficiently demonstrates that only to have been the Intent and Meaning of it. It was in these Terms, 25 *Ed.* 3. *Rot. Parl. N.* 171. " *Item, Come* les Justi-" ces nostre Seigneur le Roy *assignes en di-" verses Countees ajuggeent les Gentz que " sont empechez devant eux come* Traytors " *pur diversez causes*, desconnues a la " Comune estre Treason, *Que please a " nostre Seigneur le Roy per son Conseil, " & per les Grants & Sages de la terre, " declarer les Points de Treson en cest " present Parliament. Item*, Whereas *the " Justices of our Lord the King*, assigned " in diverse Counties, do adjudge the " People who are brought before them " as Traytors, for divers Causes *unknown " to the Commons, to be Treason.* May it please " our Lord the King, by the Advice of his " Council, and the Great and Wise Men " of the Land, to declare the Points of

" Treason,

"Treason, in this present Parliament". But to make the Force of this Observation appear the stronger, I shall state the Difference of the Method which was formerly used in the making Acts of Parliament, from that which is now in Use. Antiently, a Bill in the Nature of a Petition was delivered to the Commons, and by them sent up to the Lords, and there it was immediately entred upon the Lords Rolls, where the Royal Assent was entred also; and upon this, as a Ground Work, the Judges used at the End of the Parliament, to draw up the Substance of the Petition and Answer into the Form of a Statute, which was afterwards entred upon the Rolls, called the Statute-Rolls, which were distinct Rolls from those called the Lords Rolls, or the Parliament-Rolls. Upon the Statute-Rolls neither the Bill nor Petition from the Commons, nor Answer from the Lords, nor the Royal Assent, were entred. But only the Statute as it was modell'd and drawn up by the Judges. This was the Method till about *Henry* the 5th's Time, when it was desired that the Acts of Parliament might be drawn by the Judges before the rising of the Parliament; which was occasioned by Reason of a Complaint then made, that the Statutes were not fairly drawn after the Parliament was dissolved or prorogued. In *Henry* the 6th's

Time

Time this Method was alter'd, and Bills in the Form of an Act of Parliament were brought into the House. Upon which Bill, if the Commons approved it, was written, *Soit baile al Seigneurs*; when it came into the House of Lords they wrote upon it, *Soit baile al Roy*: Upon which was afterwards entred the King's Assent, in these Terms, *le Roy le voelt*. And this is the Method used at this Day, *Vid. Hales*, *Prynn*, *Hakewell*, Mod. Ten. Parl.

From this it is manifest, how necessary it is to peruse *the Petition* upon which a Statute is drawn, in order to understand an old Act of Parliament. By what has been said, I hope that it appears plainly, what the Mischief was against which this Act of Parliament was levell'd. And I think it can never be supposed, that the Parliament intended to confine all Treason to those particular Species which are mention'd in this Act; since it is utterly impossible to be done, for *an Act of Parliament* to determine and specifie all *Cases of Treason* in the Nature of Things, seems to be as absurd as it wou'd be to specifie *all the Actions on the Case*. I say this the more confidently, because it may be proved from the Act it self, that the makers of it thought so, for the very Reason alledged for the Clause of Reservation, is, because "that many other like Cases might "hap-

" happen in Time to come, which a Man
" cannot think nor declare at this Time.

It may justly therefore be concluded, that every Thing is even now *Treason at the Common Law*, which was so before this Statute was made: And all the difference created by it, relates wholly to the Jurisdiction of those *Courts* which are to *take Cognizance* of Crimes of this Nature. It is certain that any inferior Court of Justice cannot now adjudge any Thing to be Treason, which is not such in the plain Sense and Meaning of this, or some other subsequent Statute. But it seems to be as certain, that if any other Case does happen, which is supposed to be Treason, and is not specified in this Statute, *the Parliament* have reserved to themselves *a Power* of declaring it to be Treason; and when any such Declaration is made, the Criminal suffers as legally for a Traytor within this Statute, as if he had been condemned in *Westminster-Hall* upon any Point of Treason plainly specified in the Act.

This therefore is the State of the Case upon this Statute, that it was not the Intention of the Parliament to annihilate all such Treasons which were not specified, but only to regulate and abridge that almost discretionary Power of adjudging Treason which was in the ordinary Judges. Those particular

cular Treaſons which are certain and indiſputable, as, *e. g.* Conſpiring the King's Death, levying War againſt him in his Realm, or elſewhere, counterfeiting Money, &c. are left to the ordinary Courts of Juſtice. But thoſe other Caſes which are not ſo clear, but depend upon *Conſtructions, and neceſſary Inferences*, they thought dangerous to truſt with any Power *inferior* to that of the *Parliament*.

The next Thing to be conſidered, is an Objection which is frequently urg'd (*viz.*) That this Clauſe of Reſervation is repeal'd.

Mr. *Lane* in his Argument for my Lord *Strafford*, aſſerts roundly, that this Clauſe was repealed by 1 *H.* 4. *cap.* 10. and by 1 *M. cap.* 1. and *my Lord Clarendon* gives his *probatum eſt* to this Opinion, *p.* 177. *Vol.* 1. in *Fol.* And tells us, " *That Mr.* " Lane *averr'd this with ſuch Confidence as* " *a Man uſes who believes himſelf to be in* " *the right.*

This amounts, almoſt, to the diſputing a Matter of Fact; and in Anſwer to it, I ſhall particularly conſider the Two Statutes which are ſo much inſiſted on. The *Stat.* 1 *H.* 4. *cap.* 10. is in theſe Words, " *Whereas* in the Parliament held 21 *R.* 2. divers " Pains of Treaſon were ordained, inſomuch that no Man knew how he ought " to

" to behave himſelf, to do, ſpeak, or ſay, " for fear of ſuch Pains. It is accorded, " that in no Time to come any Treaſon be " adjudged *otherwiſe*, than as it was or- " dained by the Statute 25 *Ed.* 3.

Let any Man read this *Statute*, and then ſay if there is any Expreſſion in it that looks like a Repeal of any part of 25 *E.* 3. Or if it be not as plain a *Reſtoration and Inforcement of it in toto* as can be expreſſed in Words. And ſurely it cannot be pretended, that a Man condemn'd for a Treaſon declar'd by Parliament, in Vertue of that Clauſe of Reſervation, is adjudged *otherwiſe* than was ordained by the Statute 25 *Ed.* 3. This ſeems to be the plain Senſe and Meaning of this Statute; and it is manifeſt from the very Terms of it, that the principal Miſchief the Makers had in view, was to relieve the Subject againſt what had paſs'd in the *Parliament* 21 *R.* 2.

But it may be objected, to what end was this Statute 1 *H.* 4. made, if it does not take away thoſe Common Law Treaſons which remain'd after the Statute of 25 *Ed.* 3. Why, *Firſt*, It repeals all ſuch Treaſons as had been made by any *Statute* ſince 25 *Ed.* 3. And, *Secondly*, It takes away all the *Declaratory Treaſons in Parliament* after 25 *Ed.* 3. which was a very con-

confiderable Effect of it, fince thofe Declarations had been frequently made ufe of to oppreſs the Subject: For whenever any Declaration of Treafon was made in Parliament, the Inferiour Courts conftrued it to be *Subfidiary to the* 25 *Ed.* 3. and took upon them to act therein in fuch manner, that *toties quoties*, the like Cafe happened before them, they adjudged it to be Treafon. Againft this Grievance was the Subject relieved by this Statute. And by the way it may be obferved, that the true Reafon for the inferting a Claufe into the Act of Attainder of the Earl of *Strafford*, *fc.* (That it fhould not be drawn into Precedent) was in order to prevent a Grievance of this Nature, as appears plainly from the very Words of the Claufe. *Sc.* " Provided that no Judge or Judges, Juftice " or Juftices whatfoever, fhall adjudge, " or interpret any Act or Thing to be " Treafon; nor hear or determine any " Treafon in any other manner than he " or they fhould, or ought to have done " before the making of this Act, and as if " this Act had never been made.

2. *The Statue* 1 *Mariæ, cap.* 1. hath two Claufes in it which are to be confidered. By the *Firft*, It is Enacted, " That from " thenceforth none Act, Deed, or Offence, " *being by Act of Parliament, or Statute,* " *made*

" *made Treason*, *Petit Treason*, &c. shall
" be taken, had, deemed, or adjudged to be
" High Treason, Petit Treason, *&c.* but
" only *such as be declared to be High Treason*,
" *Petit Treason*, &c. *in or by the Act of Parliament made* 25 Ed. 3.

These are the Words; and I shall not wast Time in making particular Observations upon them, for I think it as clear as Words can make it, that this Clause extends only to the Repeal of *such Treasons* as had *been made by Act of Parliament*; so that as for any Thing contained in this Clause, the *Common Law Treasons are altogether untouch'd*, and stand upon the same footing as if this Act of Parliament had never been made.

The second Clause is in these Terms. *Sc.* " Nor that any Pains of Death, Pe-
" nalty, or Forfeiture in any wise en-
" sue, or be to any Offender or Offen-
" ders, for the doing or committing any
" High Treason, Petit Treason, *&c.* o-
" ther than such as be in the Statute
" made 25 *Ed.* 3. ordained and provi-
" ded.

I dare refer this Case to every Reader, whether there be any Thing in these Words like a Repeal of any part of the Statute 25 *Ed.* 3. for let it *intend only the Punishment of Treason*, or both

Trea-

Treason and Punishment; yet all is referr'd to the 25 *Ed.* 3. and it is plainly no more than a *Re-establishment in toto of that Statute.*

So that in Effect this Statute is the same with that 1 *H.* 4. and its Operation is nothing else but to repeal all *Statutory or Declaratory Treasons*, and Punishments made subsequent to the Statute 25 *Ed.* 3.

But farther; is it possible to conceive, that my Lord Chief Justice *Coke*, who must certainly be allowed to know whether a Statute be repeal'd, or not, shou'd in his Comentary upon this very Statute 25 *Ed.* 3. include this Clause of Reservation as a subsisting part of the Statute, was it not still in Force? He even particularly tells us, what is a *Declaration of Treason* within this Statute, and what is not (*viz*) that it must be done by the whole *Parliament*, *King*, *Lords*, *and Commons*. And he adds, in order to enforce his Opinion, that the Declaration and Judgment of the Lords against Sir *Thomas Talbot*, for conspiring the Death of the *Dukes of* Lancaster *and* Gloucester, *the King's Uncles*, was illegal and void, for want of the *Concurrence of the Commons*, without which it cou'd not be said to be a Declaration of Treason by Par-

Parliament, *Rot. Par.* 17 *R.* 2. *n.* 20. Vid. *& Cokes 3d Inſtit. pa.* 22.

In his Opinion therefore the Clauſe ſtands unrepeal'd, and if it muſt be underſtood (as he thinks it ought) ſo as to relate to the whole Parliament, King, Lords, and Commons, the Clauſe is then manifeſtly, only *affirmatory of that Power* which it is not poſſible to ſuppoſe a *Parliament to be without*; for ſurely no Man can pretend to diſpute, but that the Parliament muſt always have a Right to inflict upon any Criminal *even ex poſt facto* ſuch Puniſhment as they may think his Crime deſerves, altho' *this reſervatory Clauſe* had never been inſerted into the Act of Parliament.

If this therefore be allowed to be the Caſe, it ſeems to be of very little Conſequence, whether this Clauſe be repealed or not; And I ſhould not have ſpent ſo much Time to prove that in Fact it was not, had I not obſerved that a great Number of People imagined it to be of the utmoſt Conſequence. *For if it is ſtill in Force, it is certain that it can give no additional Right to the Parliament*; *and if it is repealed, it can take nothing away.*

The Insignificancy of the Clause in this Sense of it, has among other Reasons, inclin'd some Persons to think that it does not relate to the whole Parliament, but that the *House of Lords*, with the King's concurring Assent, have (or at least had) a Power to declare what is Treason, and what is not, within this Statute. *The Form of the Petition, and the Answer to it,* to them seems to favour that Opinion, (*viz.*) 'That 'the Right of Declaring and Judging what 'is High-Treason in Parliament, did origi- 'nally belong to the King, with the Con- 'currence of the House of Lords, exclusive 'of the House of Commons, at whose Re- 'quest this Declaration of the Articles of 'Treason was made. For, say they, the Petition did not contain particularly what Points shou'd be declared to be Treason, but was only in general Terms, That the Points of Treason might be settled in certain. *The Declaration* of Treason in particular Cases, seems also to have something in it more of the *Judicial* than the *Legislative Capacity*; and they cannot see any Reason why the Word (*Parliament*) used in the Clause, shou'd create so vast a Difference; all the Proceedings in the House of Lords being stiled *Placita coram Rege in Parliamento.* And yet no one ever pretended to infer from thence, a Necessity of the Concurrence of the *House of Commons* in their *Judicial* Acts.

In Fact, the House of Lords have in particular Cases, with the Consent of the King, adjudged several Persons to die as Traitors, for *Crimes* which were not *Treason* within the Statute 25 *Ed.* 3. And notwithstanding what *my Lord Chief Justice Coke* says, 4 *Instit. Pag.* 23. I do not believe it was ever assigned in Parliament as Error, that the House of Commons were not concurrent to the Judgment: The Case which the *Chief Justice* refers to, to justify this Assertion, is that of *Thomas Montague*, Earl of *Sarum*, 2. *H.* 5. *Rot. Parl. N.* 13, 14. who Petitioned in Parliament to have a Judgment reversed that was given against his Father, 2. *H.* 4. *N*° 30, 31. But he did not in his Petition assign any such Error as is pretended. And if he had, I cannot see how it could support what is concluded from it, but rather directly the contrary, since that Petition was rejected, and consequently all the Errors assigned in it were disallowed.

I know very well that the concurrent Jurisdiction (in some Cases) of the Commons in Points of Judicature, is a Favourite Opinion, *Et non nostrum est tantas componere lites.* However, it is wonderful to me, that the Chief-Justice shou'd quote a Record by way of Proof, which was nothing to the Purpose, and

and omit another of a much antienter Date, which to me ſeems to be almoſt in Point. *King Ed.* 3. *Anno* 1° *Regni ſui*, wrote a Letter to the Pope, giving an Account of the Death of *Edmund* Earl of *Kent*, wherein after having made a Relation of the ſeveral heinous Crimes which were objected to him, he uſes theſe Words, (*viz.*) " *Nos igitur* " *tanta facinora, ex relatione fideli ipſorum* " *Comitum Baronum & magnatum Cognoſ-* " *centes eiſdem Comitibus Baronibus Magnati-* " *bus & aliis de Communitate Regni injunximus* " *ut Super hiis diſcernerent, & judicarent,* " *Quod rationi & Juſtitiæ conveniret habendo* " *præ Oculos Solum Deum.* Qui eum Con- " corde & Unanimi Sententiâ tanquam reum " Criminis læſæ Majeſtatis morti adjudi- " carunt, Cui Sententiæ, *&c. Rim. Fæd.* " 4 *Tom. Pag.* 424.

The Precedents of the Lords having exerciſed this Power (according to Mr. *Prynn*, in his Plea for that Noble Houſe) are numerous; ſome of which the Reader may himſelf obſerve, among thoſe which I ſhall be obliged to mention, to prove, that ever ſince this famous Statute has been made, Perſons of all Ranks have been executed as Traitors, for Facts which were not ſpecified in it.

A° 1*R.* 1. *N*° 38, 39, 40. *Rot. Parl.* The Commons prayed, that all thoſe Cap-

 tains

tains who had rendred or loſt Towns or Caſtles through Default, might be put to Anſwer it in Parliament, and ſeverely puniſhed according to their Deſerts, by the Award of the Lords and Barons. Upon which *William de Weſton*, and *John de Gomenez*, were brought before the Lords by the Conſtable of the *Tower*, in whoſe Cuſtody they were Priſoners, and were Queſtioned for having Surrendred the Caſtles of *Outherwyke* and *Ardes* to the *French*, without a ſufficient Warrant. There was nothing of Corruption or Treachery prov'd againſt them, but what they did, ſeem'd to proceed entirely from Cowardice, (which I ſuppoſe no-body imagines to be Treaſon within the Statute) yet for an Example to other Commanders, they were by the Lords, both adjudged to die as Traitors.

20 *R.* 2. *N.* 15, 16. 23. *R. P.* Sir *Thomas Haxey*, Clerk, was by the King and Lords in Parliament, adjudged to die as a Traitor, and to forfeit all his Lands, Goods, Chattels, *&c.* for exhibiting to the Houſe of Commons a Scandalous Bill againſt the King and his Court, for moderating the *outragious Expences cauſed by Biſhops and Ladies*, &c. Indeed 1 *H.* 4. upon the Petition of the ſaid *Haxey*, ſupported by a Petition from the Houſe of Commons in his Favour, that Judgment againſt him was reverſed, by the Advice

vice and Consent of the Lords Spiritual and Temporal.

22 *R.* 2. *N.* 28. *The Duke of Hereford*, after Judgment was given against him at *Coventry*, had procured by Letters Patents from the King, that he might, during his Absence, by his Attorneys, Sue and have Liveries of any Lands descended to him, and his Homage respited; which Letters Patents were revoked in Parliament, as contrary to Law. And *Henry Bowet*, Clerk, for being of Counsel to this Device made by the *Duke of Hereford*, was by the Lords adjudged to die, and forfeit as a Traitor. It would be too long to Transcribe all the Presidents of the Lords taking upon themselves singly to adjudge Persons to die as Traitors, for Facts which were not Treason, within the Statute of 25 *Ed.* 3. It is visible from these recited Precedents, that the Lords did take upon them to pronounce Judgments of this Nature. It matters not much, whether the Lords acted *eo nomine*, as having a declaratory Power of what was or was not Treason, when the Criminals were in Fact hang'd as Traitors upon such Judgments. In all these Cases, the Commons were look'd upon as altogether unconcern'd in them; and presently after the before-quoted Judgments had been pronounced, it was declared in full Parliament, *Anno* 1° *ipsius H.* 4. *N.* 79.

" *That the Commons were only Petitioners,*
" *and that* all Judgments did appertain to
" the *King, and to the Lords* ; and that the
" Concurrence of the House of Commons
" was no ways necessary, *unless it were to*
" *Statutes, Grants, Subsidies, and such like.*

This Declaration is in some measure an Affirmance of the Judicature they had formerly execised; and their subsequent Practice was conformable to it; as in the Case of Sir *John Mortimer* 2° *H.* 6. who being sent to the *Tower*, upon Suspition of Treason against *H.* 5. broke his Prison, and made his Escape; for which he was indicted of Treason, and the *Indictment was return'd into Parliament*, and there confirmed. Being afterwards apprehended, he was actually Sentenced upon this Indictment, and Executed as a Traytor, without so much as an Arraignment or Tryal.

This Confirmation was Parliamentary, and yet the Bishops are not Parties to it: it begins thus, *de advisamento dict. Dominor'. temporalium ac ad requisicon' totius Communitat. &c.* So clear a Proof of Guilt was slight esteemed to be in those Times, *R. P.* 2 *H.* 6. N° 18. 22. *R.* 2. *Thomas Arundel*, Archbishop of *Canterbury*, was adjudged a Traytor by the King and Lords upon the Accusation of the Commons; for that, when he was *Chancellor*, he procured and executed a Com-

Commiſſion, which they alledg'd to be trayterouſly made. *The Great Seal* it ſelf cou'd not ſecure this Miniſter; and yet, ſurely *its Authority is equal to a forc'd, tho' pretendedly equitable Conſtruction of a Sign Manual.*

17. *Rich.* 2. The bare conſpiring the Death of the Duke of *Lancaſter*, was by King and Lords adjudged to be Treaſon, 1 *H.* 4. *R. C. N.* 11. to 17. *John Hall* being in Cuſtody of the Marſhal of *England*, was by him brought before the Lords in Parliament, and there charg'd by *Walter Clapton, then Lord Chief Juſtice*, by the King's Command, with being concern'd in the Murther of the Duke of *Glouceſter*, who was ſmother'd to Death between Featherbeds at *Calais*, by the Command of K. *R.* 2. *John Hall* confeſſed the whole Tranſaction at large, which was put in writing by *James Billingford*, then Clerk of the Crown, and was read to the Lords; and upon hearing, the King and all the Temporal *Lords* in Parliament, reſolv'd, That the ſaid *John Hall* did by his own Confeſſion deſerve to ſuffer as ſevere a Death as they cou'd adjudge him to, becauſe the Duke of *Glouceſter* was ſo high a Perſon. And thereupon *toutz les Seigneurs temporalz, par aſſent du Roy*, did adjudge him to be hang'd, drawn, and quarter'd, &c. So that in this Caſe the Lords in Parliament paſſed a Judgment of High-Treaſon againſt a Commoner,

moner, for no other Crime but the Murther of a Great Peer.

This way of proceeding by *the House of Lords singly*, as it was very liable to Objection, it was soon laid aside; but then the whole Parliament jointly acted the same Things, and supply'd their Jurisdiction by proceeding in Consequence of that declaratory Power reserved 25 *Ed.* 3. by way of Bill. As 3° *R.* 2. for a farther Declaration of Treasons, it was adjudged by the Temporal Justices, and afterwards confirm'd by Parliament; That whereas one *John Imperiall*, who was come as an Ambassador to the King (and was thereby under his Protection) to treat of an Alliance to be had and made between the King, and the *Duke and Comonalty of Genoa*, was Murther'd in *London* by *Kirby* and *Grove*: Such Act and Murther was Treason, and a Fault of the King's Royal Majesty impaired.

There is nothing in this Case which cou'd possibly bring it within the Statute of *Ed.* 3. without the Honour of the Nation was concern'd that the publick Faith shou'd be kept. The Parliament, therefore did not think themselves obliged to *make a Law first*; but they made the *first Criminal an Example.*

But what was the reason of this Case? For it is that which in reality is the Law, and must govern us in our search after Treason;

ſon. For if no Caſe can be concluded from Precedents to be treaſonable, but only ſuch as exactly Parallel and Quadrate in every Circumſtance, Precedents are of no manner of uſe, ſince perhaps there *never were two Caſes exactly alike.*

The reaſon was, certainly, becauſe the Murther of an Ambaſſador being ſo high a Violation of the Law of Nations, gave to the Common-Wealth of *Genoa, a juſt Cauſe of War againſt the King and his Kingdom.*

By this Rule, therefore, every Action which a Subject Commits, or is Acceſſory to, which may give a Foreign Nation a juſt Cauſe of War againſt his own Country, is treaſonable. This ſeems to be almoſt ſelf-evident; and if we apply it, what muſt we think of ſuch Miniſters, who in Defiance to the *Laws of Nations and natural Juſtice,* adviſe a Sovereign *to violate publick Faith,* and Arbitrarily, without any Reaſon aſſigned, to declare themſelves abſolv'd from the moſt Solemn Engagements with antient Allies? *Can it be Treaſon to Correſpond only with old Enemies, and yet juſtifiable to create new?*

11° *R.* 2. *Robert de Vere* Duke of *Ireland, Nevil,* Arch biſhop of *York*; *Treſilian,* and others, were attainted of High-Treaſon, for deſigning to ſubvert the Laws of the Kingdom: The Articles againſt them are very remarkable,

remarkable, but much too long to be tranſcribed.

Treſilian, *Belknap*, and ſeveral other *Lawyers* were adjudged Traytors, for delivering an Opinion (when they were demanded by the King) contrary to, and in Subverſion of the Law of *England*. To give the Reader a Notion of what Doctrines were then in Parliament thought Treaſonable, I ſhall briefly State two or three of the Queſtions propoſed by the King, with theſe Gentlemen's Anſwers.

Q. 1. It was demanded, Whether after the Parliament was met, and the Buſineſs of the Kingdom, and Cauſes of ſummoning the Parliament declared; if the King propoſed Articles, upon which he ſhou'd Inſiſt the Lords and Commons ought to proceed, and the Lords and Commons ſhou'd refuſe to go upon the King's Articles, until they proceeded upon other Articles of their own.

Q. Whether the King was not ſo far the Maſter of his Parliament, as that they were obliged to go upon his Articles firſt? To this Queſtion theſe Judges anſwered, That in ſuch Caſe the King ought to have the Government, and if any one preſum'd to act to the contrary, he was to be puniſhed as a Traytor. There was a long Diſpute upon this very Point in the firſt Parliament that met, *Anno* 1640. K. *Charles* 1. inſiſted by variety

riety of Messages and Speeches made by Lord-Keeper *Finch*, that they should preferably to all other Business proceed to vote him a Supply, promising them, that they should sit long enough to dispatch any other Business they shou'd think fit to go upon: *The Commons refused* to comply with this desire of the King's, and insisted, that they ought to be at Liberty to proceed upon and remonstrate their Grievances, before they entred upon any other Business. After long disputing, they were at last dissolved in Anger for their Non-compliance in this Particular. And yet, my Lord *Clarendon* in his History, Vol. 1. Page 110. in Fol. owns, "*It cou'd not be hop'd that more Sober, or "Dispassionate Men shou'd ever meet together, "and that it was not possible to imagine what "Offence they had given to incite the King to "that Resolution*; Vid. Rush. Coll. p. 1114. to 1155.

Q. 2. It was demanded, whether, when the King thought fit to remove any of his Judges or other Officers, and to punish them, those Officers might be *Impeached in Parliament* for their Offences, *without the King's Consent*. They answer'd, they could not, and that if any one acted to the Contrary, he was to be punished as a Traytor.

3. It was demanded, how he was to be punish'd, who mov'd in Parliament, that *the Statute*

Statute might be ſent for, by which *Edw.* 2. the King's great Grandfather, was adjudged in Parliament, by the Inſpection of which Statute the new Statute Ordinance and Commiſſion were conceiv'd? They unanimouſly anſwered, That as well he who ſo mov'd, as the other, who by pretext of that Motion, carried that Statute to the Parliament, were to be puniſhed as Traytors.

N. B. The Articles of Impeachment againſt theſe Perſons, are Printed in *Henry de Knighton de Even. Angl. intra Scriptores decem.* p. 2713. to 2727. The Queſtions propoſed to the Judges, are in *pag.* 2694.

It is true that theſe Attainders were revers'd, *Anno* 21 *R.* 2. But then that whole Parliament almoſt was again revers'd, *p.* 1. *H.* 4. And in *that very Parliament which reduced Treaſons to the Statute of* Edw. 3. theſe Attainders were confirm'd and made good, and are (I believe) in force unto this Day.

About this time the Method of proceeding in Parliament began to change; and inſtead of Indictments being firſt found againſt the Parties, and then return'd into Parliament, they have generally choſen to act in the way of Bill, as being the Method leaſt liable to Doubts and Objections, and at the ſame time moſt uſeful and expeditious in thoſe Circumſtances, when the Neceſſities of the State

State *may require some exemplary Act of Justice.* And I believe that for 300 Years past, no Person has been Attainted in Parliament for any Treason not specifyed in the Statute 25 *Edw.* 3. otherwise than by Bill; which clearly evinces that way of Proceeding to be *as Parliamentary*, as any other can possibly be shewn to be. To enumerate all the Instances of Persons who have been in Parliament Attainted for Treason, by Bill, wou'd be endless. Indeed no Man pretends to controvert the Fact; it is universally known that *this Act of Supreme Power* has been frequently exercised in almost every Reign. But one or two Acts of Attainder having pass'd, which some People apprehend to be unjust, and not to have had sufficient Foundation to support them, they from thence have *taken up a Notion*, that the very Power it self is naturally unjust.

It may be observed to be the *Humour* of *England*, that whenever any thing by abuse grows to be a Grievance to the People (be it in it self never so useful and necessary for the Support of Government) they can think of no other Remedy, but by taking the whole entirely away. They never so much as attempt *to correct and restore it to its Original Use.* But when the Want of it is felt, they supply it with some new Law, which is frequently

quently attended with Conſequences much more grievous than the Miſchiefs they reliev'd themſelves from. *The Court of Star-Chamber*, whilſt kept within due bounds, was certainly of the greateſt Uſe to preſerve the Peace and Security of the Kingdom; and perhaps was the only Court, which by its *ordinary and proper Juriſdiction*, could effectually *prevent and puniſh Riots*, Perjuries and other Miſdemeanors of the higheſt Nature: But being made uſe of by the Court to ſupport Proclamations and Orders of State, and to vindicate Illegal Commiſſions and Monopolies, that Extenſion of their Power became a Grievance inſupportable; and the Nation was never eaſy till that Court was entirely ſuppreſs'd by Act of Parliament. *The Houſe of Commons* were ſo eager in their Zeal to deſtroy what they called *a Court of Inquiſition*, that tho' the Bill was of ſo great Conſequence, yet they ſent it up to the Lords, with only once reading it, and without its being ever committed, which was a thing perhaps never before heard of in Parliament, *Cla. v.* 1. 223. At the Reſtauration *of King Charles* II. this National Diſpoſition appeared in variety of Inſtances; People were become ſo weary of the Miſeries they had groan'd under, during the time of the *Uſurpation*, that they univerſally conceiv'd the

utmoſt

utmoſt Deteſtation and Abhorrence of all thoſe Proceedings which they apprehended had been in any manner conducive to bring them upon them. But then it was with ſo little diſtinction and reſerve, that it became Faſhionable (and almoſt neceſſary) to ſhew their Zeal to the King, by thinking and acting in every particular, contrary to thoſe Men who had in ſome meaſure brought on the Civil Wars. And it was then (as it ſtill is) a ſufficient Reaſon, with a great number of Men, to condemn any Principle or Proceeding, if they did but believe *it had been profeſſed or practiſed* by the Parliament in 1641. Every one knows that *the Earl of Strafford* was Attainted by Act of Parliament in *Cha.* 1*ſt*'s time, and that his Attainder was, after the Reſtoration, revers'd by Parliament. That Earl's Caſe was commonly thought to be very hard: For conſidering the particular Defence which he made to every Article; and that *no one Fact* was prov'd clearly againſt him, which was in it ſelf Treaſon, People generally concluded, that Perſonal Malice againſt the Earl, or ſome other ſiniſter Deſign, was more conſulted in that Proſecution, than the Deſire or Love of Juſtice. This *Act of Attainder* has now for Fifty Years been conſtantly repreſented to the People as the higheſt Act of Injuſtice, and with great

Manage-

Management and Induſtry (few Miniſters loving that Doctrine which leads a Parliament to examine into and puniſh their Miſdemeanors in ſo ſevere and extraordinary a manner) they have inſtilled and propagated in the Minds of Men a diſeſteem (and almoſt hatred) of *that Power* which is ſo often neceſſary to prevent the Ruin of their Country, or *to puniſh Criminals who have attempted it*, and which their Fathers prided and valued themſelves in the Poſſeſſion of. To remove this Prejudice, I ſhall therefore briefly endeavour to ſhew the natural Juſtice of Bills of Attainder, and then conclude this Paper.

A Bill of Attainder may in ſome Senſe be ſtyl'd a *Parliamentary Judgment*. The Supreme Legiſlative Power of the Nation, by it exempts the particular Caſe of a notorious Criminal from thoſe Courts, and from thoſe Rules which are appointed for the Tryal of the Generality of Caſes, and inflict a Puniſhment upon him adequate to the Crime they are convinc'd he is guilty of. However, this manner of proceeding being but a *Mode of Puniſhment*, to ſhew the natural Juſtice of it, it will be neceſſary to conſider, how the Right or Power of Puniſhment is derived to the *publick Part* of any Society.

All

All Authors allow, that in the State of Nature, every Individual had a Right to defend, either his Perſon or Property, by all neceſſary Means whatſoever, when it cannot otherwiſe be affected, even by the Death of the Aggreſſor. From this Principle *Solely*, have ſome endeavour'd to derive the Right of puniſhing to the Magiſtrate. But to me, it does not ſeem to be a ſufficient Foundation, for the whole Extent of *Political Power*. Let it be, therefore, farther conſidered, that the State of Nature is not without a Law. *Reaſon is that Law.* And that teaches, That all Men being naturally equal; no Man ought to prejudice another, either in his *Perſon or Property*; but on the contrary, they ought to aſſiſt one another by all means juſtifiable. For as the Law of Nature willeth the Peace and Preſervation of all Mankind, every Man is equally concern'd in the Obſervation of it: And therefore, that all Men might be reſtrain'd from acting contrary to it; the Execution of the Law of Nature is in that State veſted *in every Man*; and in Conſequence of that Law, every Man may Puniſh (that is, inflict a Pain upon) every Tranſgreſſor of it, to ſuch a Degree, as may hinder its Violation for the future. For the Law of Nature, like all other Laws, wou'd be in vain, was there no Body in that State who had a Right to make the *Obſervation* of it

H more

more obviouſly the Intereſt of every Individual, *than the Tranſgreſſion.* And if in the State of Nature, *any one Man* can puniſh an Offender for an Offence or Injury done to another, *every one may.*

From theſe two Principles united, the Power of the Sword is *fully* deriv'd to the Magiſtrate. Society is form'd by the Conſent of Particulars, and muſt neceſſarily be ſuppos'd to have been intended for the mutual Good of every individual Member of which it is compoſed. The *Right of the whole,* is the Sum of the Rights of *every Individual* ; and conſequently the Whole can be poſſeſs'd of no Right ; but what, in ſome manner, reſided in each particular, who muſt be ſuppoſed, to have granted over to the Society as ſuch, every Right which it is inconſiſtent for him to retain in a Social State. And therefore, as every Individual in the State of Nature has an abſolute Right to defend himſelf from all Attempts whatſoever ; *and likewiſe, as* every Individual has an abſolute Right, or is rather under a ſort of Obligation to exact the Obſervation of the Law of Nature from every Man, and to aſſiſt the injur'd Perſon againſt the Oppreſſor: *By every Individual's* departing for himſelf from each of theſe Rights, both of them are entirely transferr'd to *the Society as ſuch,* and from *thence to the Magiſtrate,* or Perſons veſted

vested with the *Legislative and Executive* Power. And therefore, whatsoever is absolutely necessary to the Preservation of the *Society as such*, the *Legislative part* of it can justify the doing. And whatever Punishment, Fine, *&c.* is but equal to the Injury or Damage done to the Society as such, or necessary to prevent its being attempted for the Future, they may justly inflict. For surely it is the heighth of Absurdity to imagine a Government under an Obligation to afford Protection and Reparation *to any one Individual*; and yet, at the same time under a moral Incapacity of affording it to *all the Individuals* considered together *as one Body*.

But these Observations may, perhaps appear too general; it will be necessary therefore to consider the Force of the Objections made to this Doctrine. The Strength of them, as has been before observed, amounts to this: That the explicite Laws of every Society being the Standard, if not of Right and Wrong, at least of what is punishable or unpunishable, therefore *Bills of Attainder* are unjust, because it is the punishing a Person for Actions which he had reason to think himself *secure* in doing.

This Proposition destroys the very Notion of Right and Wrong, and makes the whole of Morality to be *purely Accidental and Po-*

 litical.

litical. But ſurely there is ſomething elſe requiſite to Juſtice, beſides a *bare Eſtabliſhment*: Let us therefore examine it to the bottom, and ſee how far a Government is obliged to give every Individual Notice for what he is, or is not to be puniſhed.

Right, abſtractedly conſidered, is previous too, and perfectly diſtinct from all Human Eſtabliſhment: It ariſes from that *neceſſary Relation* which the Actions of one Rational Agent bear to another. When they are conſonant to thoſe mutual Obligations all Mankind are naturally under, they are denominated Juſt; when contrary, Unjuſt. This is Natural Reaſon; and Society can only give an additional Sanction to theſe *eternal Laws of Action*, by the inflicting effectual Rewards and Puniſhments: It is abſolutely impoſſible to make them either more or leſs Juſt. But then *ſubſequent to Society*, a new Species of Right and Wrong has been introduced; ſo that thoſe Actions which are *Mala in ſe*, or naturally Evil, muſt be carefully diſtinguiſh'd from thoſe which are *Mala quia prohibita*, or Evil by reaſon of ſome Social or other Eſtabliſhment. This Diſtinction ſeems to ſolve the whole Difficulty, ſince it is univerſally allowed to be an Injuſtice in any Government, to puniſh the latter ſort, without a due previous Notice, (indeed to ſpeak exactly, no Action of that Nature is unjuſt,

unjuſt, till the Law prohibiting them is ſufficiently promulg'd.) And of the former ſort there are Crimes ſo ſhocking, that all Mankind muſt agree, they ought to be capitally puniſhed, altho' there were not any *written Laws in the Univerſe*. It is not poſſible that any Legiſlature whatever ſhou'd be able to provide for all future Contingencies; ſuch monſtrous Crimes are frequently committed, that they are not provided againſt, becauſe the Government did not imagine Mankind to be capable of them? Does it therefore follow, the Criminal is not to be puniſh'd who *firſt ventur'd* to commit them? For a conſiderable time among the *Romans*, there was no Law againſt Parricide; was it therefore unjuſt to diſtinguiſh *the firſt Man* who durſt venture on ſo monſtrous a Crime, by a Puniſhment extraordinary? Before the 22. *H*. 8. *c*. 9. there was no particular Law in *England* againſt poyſoning, was it therefore unjuſt by Bill of Attainder to make an Example of the *firſt Man* who introduc'd ſo deteſtable a Villany? Setting Fire to one of the King's Ships is not Treaſon within the Statute 25 *Edw*. 3. yet cou'd any one think it unjuſt, ſhou'd the Parliament *by Bill Attaint* the Perſon of *High-Treaſon*, who ſhou'd ſet Fire to the whole Royal Navy? For after all, a Man's being Attainted by Bill of High-Treaſon, amounts to no more than a Declaration of the Supreme Power, That the Crime the Person is guilty of deserves the Punishment assigned to those Crimes which are commonly known by the Name of High-Treason. Neither is it unusual for that Term, to signify no more than a designation of Punishment. As, *e. g.* it is High-Treason in *Ireland*, wilfully to commit Murder, to burn a Stack of Corn, Hay, *&c.*

Crimes of this magnitude no Man can pretend to be ignorant of; they never were committed, but the Criminal was Conscious of the Injustice of what he did. And therefore no *previous Notice* is necessary to justify his Punishment; for the only Reason which makes Notice necessary to the punishing Crimes of the other Nature, is, because no Man *can know* whether such a particular Action be Criminal, until he be informed of its being prohibited.

If this Doctrine therefore be true in respect to the Cases above-mentioned, much more is it so when apply'd to those Crimes which affect Mankind in a higher manner.

The Punishment surely ought to bear some proportion to the Injury: The greatest Enemies to Bills of Attainder wou'd acquiesce under them, were they only applied to the Punishment of *Murderers, Poysoners, Parricides*, &c. They wou'd not in such Cases object

ject to the Proceeding, as being *ex post facto*. The natural Villany of such Crimes is so evident, no Man cou'd be found absurd enough to affirm, the Criminal ought not to be capitally punish'd, because no explicite Law of the Society was *nominally* pronounc'd against so great a Crime *previous to its Commission*. How then can they oppose the Exercise of this Power against Crimes of so superior a Nature? Are they not equally Evident? Are they not equally contrary to the Law of Nature? They differ in nothing but the *Extent of their Mischief*. All Actions, which *no Law* whatsoever can make Just, must necessarily be Evil in themselves, and therefore may justly be punish'd by the Supreme Power of every Society, whenever they are committed, although no particular Law should be provided against them. It is the Law which is the *Bond* of Society, and creates that Political Tye which is between the Subject and the Sovereign. It is by that the Government subsists; that each Individual enjoys *Security*, *Property*, *and even Liberty it self:* Take that away, the Government is at an End, Society is dissolv'd, and Mankind, become mutual Enemies to one another, are liable to all the Mischiefs incident to such a State. It is therefore *Treason from the very Nature of Things*, for any Man to attempt the *Subversion of that Law* he is Born

Subject to. No Law *can justify* such an Action? The Punishment of it is *absolutely necessary to the Preservation of Government*; and if it cannot be done in the ordinary Methods of Proceedings, the Law of Self-Defence legitimates *any other*, tho' never so extraordinary. For there is no way under Heaven of preventing Crimes which Human Prudence cannot foresee, but by making an Example of every Man who shall commit them. My Lord *Clarendon* himself was so far convinc'd that this was High-Treason, that he carried up an Impeachment from the Commons to the Lords, against Three Barons of the Exchequer, for the Opinions they had given in the Case of Ship-Money, which the *House of Commons had voted to be in Subversion of the Law of* England. It never was thought that the delivering a false Opinion in Point of Law (which may proceed from Ignorance as well as Corruption) was High-Treason within any Statute; and yet upon the delivery of the Articles against them, he made *as warm a Speech* to the House of Lords, *as the greatest Champion for accumulative Treason*, Rush. *Coll.* Vol. 5. p. 333.

This therefore being the State of the Case, I think it needless to make any particular Application of this Doctrine to the late Transactions. It is not the Business of particular Persons in their private Capacity, to pronounce

pronounce this or that Perſon guilty of ſuch high Crimes. But I think every Man ought to be convinc'd, that the Supreme Powers of every Society, have not only a Right, but are under an actual Obligation to take Care, *Ne quid detrimenti Reſpublica capiat.* If the Principles before laid down, are once admitted to be true, every Reader, with very little Reflection, will be able to make proper Concluſions. For as every Society, as has been ſaid, is form'd by the Conſent of Particulars, ſo it neceſſarily follows from thence, that every Individual engages himſelf to do all that he is able to ſupport it; and to ſubmit his Perſon, and all that he has, in Proportion with the other Members, to the Diſpoſition of the Supreme Legiſlative Power. It is viſible that no Society can be maintained without ſuch Engagement. And therefore *it is Treaſon from the very Nature of Things,* for any Man to do any Thing *animo lædendi,* which may turn to the Prejudice of the Society of which he is a Member. And it being impoſſible to foreſee all the various Methods by which a Society may be prejudic'd, it is likewiſe impoſſible, by any poſitive Law, to prohibit them; and therefore it is juſt even *ex poſt facto,* to puniſh ſuch Crimes whenever they ſhall be committed; ſince every Man muſt neceſſarily be ſuppoſed to know that they

they are Criminal. Neither can it be objected to this Method of Proceeding *by Bill of Attainder*, that the Party concern'd is not allowed every Privilege which is essential to a fair Trial; for all that any Criminal is entitled to by the Laws of natural Justice, is a Liberty to make his full Defence; and if every Thing *necessary to that End*, be allowed him, he can have no Reason to complain. And it is notorious, that whenever any private Bill is depending in Parliament, any Man, upon Suggestion that he is a Party concern'd in Interest, in the Success of the Bill, may be heard by Counsel against it; *much more therefore, will it be allowed* any Man, against a Bill of so high a Nature as that of *Attainder*. And in Fact it was allow'd in the Case of Sir *John Fenwick*. This I look upon to be a sufficient Answer to this Objection. As to the Methods of Proceeding in Bills of Attainder, and what is, or is not, to be admitted as Evidence upon such Occasions, *&c.* 'tis a Subject much too long to be meddled with in this Paper, and wou'd very well deserve a distinct Treatise. Only this in General may be observ'd, That the Method of trying Criminals, and the Rules for examining whether any Person be guilty, or not, are *different* in almost all Nations. But it is universally agreed, and so accounted in all

Laws,

Laws, that whatſoever makes the *Truth evident*, is *ſufficient Evidence.* So that when it is agreed, that the Crime any Perſon is charged with, deſerves the higheſt Puniſhment, every Man concern'd (provided that by the Evidence produc'd, *&c.* he is in Conſcience convinc'd, that the Perſon accuſed is guilty) acts juſtly, and as he is obliged to do, when he gives his Conſent to a Bill of Attainder. For that certainly muſt be *ſufficient Evidence* to me, which induces me to *believe the Fact.*

To conclude therefore: The whole of what has been ſaid, may in ſhort be ſumm'd up thus: That *High-Treaſon* being at the Common Law, (*any horrible Offence done,* animo lædendi, *againſt the Security of either King or Kingdom,*) and the Judges in the common Courts of Law, having the entire Cognizance of it; they, in order to *ſecure conſiderable Forfeitures* to the Crown, and improve their *own Intereſt* at Court, manag'd that almoſt Diſcretionary Power, which they neceſſarily had in the Adjudication of conſtructive (or ſuch) Treaſons, which depend upon Inferences from Facts, that it became an intolerable Grievance to the Subject: To remedy which, the Statute 25 *Ed.* 3. was made, and thereby the Juriſdiction of the ordinary Courts at Law is limitted and confin'd to the particular Caſes

Cafes of Treafon, fpecified in that or fome other fubfequent Statute.

It appears manifeftly by the Petition of the Commons, upon which the Statute was made, that this Abufe in the Judges, was the Mifchief againft which it was levell'd. And it is evident from the very Terms of the Statute, that the Intention of the Legiflators was not *to annihilate* all the Treafons at Common Law, except thofe mentioned in it, but only to abridge this Jurifdiction of the Judges: Since by a particular Claufe, the Punifhment of all other Cafes of Treafon is *exprefly referv'd* to the Parliament. And the Reafon affign'd for this Claufe of Refervation is, becaufe it *is impoffible* to enumerate all Cafes of Treafon. And in Fact, Treafon may be committed fo many various Ways, and depends upon *fo many Contingencies*, that it is abfurd to imagine any prefent Set of Legiflators can by any pofitive Law, *nominally* provide againft them.

This therefore being the Nature of the Thing, the Claufe of Refervation, is only *in Affirmance* of that Power, which no Parliament can ever be fuppofed to be without. And the Difpute whether the Claufe be repealed or not, is quite out of the Queftion, and I infifted upon its not being in Fact repeal'd, (as will appear to every one who

confiders

confiders the Terms of the Statutes 1. *H.* 4. *c.* 10. and 1° *Ma. Reg. cap.* 1.) only to obviate and prevent any plaufible Objection which might be made.

This Act of Parliament therefore extends no farther than to regulate and abridge the Jurifdiction of the Inferior Courts of Juftice; And Treafon in it felf is juft as it was before this Act of Parliament was made; only with this Difference, that the Common-Judges are bound down to fuch Cafes as are fpecify'd in this or fome other Statute; and the Punifhment of conftructive or other Treafons is referved entirely to the Parliament, as being dangerous to be trufted with any *Subordinate Power.* And the Parliament has, in Fact, always exercifed this extraordinary Power in every Age, nay, in every Reign almoft, feveral Perfons have been condemn'd and executed as Traytors, for Facts not fpecify'd in this or any other Statute.

Indeed, formerly Bills have been found for any of thefe extraordinary Facts by a Common Jury, and then return'd into Parliament for a Determination: but this Method of proceeding has been long altered, and for 350 Years paft, no Man has been executed for any Treafon of this Nature, otherwife than by *Bill of Attainder.* It is no manner of Objection to fay, that this is making

making a new Law, on purpose to hang a particular Person; for so long as the Criminal has every Thing allowed him that is essential to the making his Defence, he can have no reason to complain. And it is certain, that any Man concern'd may be heard by Council, or otherwise, at the Bar of either House against such a Bill: The Method of proceeding against any Criminal is in its own Nature variable; and therefore it is ridiculous to except to this; since the Parliament, as such, consisting of different Parts, has *no Method* of expressing any Determination, &c. but by *Bill* passing both Houses, and the Royal Assent. It can be but Repetition to repeat the Reasons why the Exercise of this Power is naturally just. That every Man who commits a *Crime in its own Nature Evil*, shou'd receive a Punishment adequate to it, is so *manifestly reasonable*; and that a Supreme Legislative Power shou'd be bound down by Forms from inflicting Punishments upon such Crimes as affect the very Being of Government it self, and make their Punishment absolutely necessary to its Preservation, is *manifestly so absurd*, that it would be losing Time to say any more concerning it.

I think I need add no more. If the Judges before the Statute 25 *Ed.* 3. had a Power to punish any Man as a Traytor, for any Fact which

which they apprehended was done with a deſign to *prejudice the Publick as ſuch* : The *Parliament* by taking it away, ſhow manifeſtly, That that Power was derived from themſelves, and muſt therefore *neceſſarily* be inherent in them.

What I have now written, as it was ſincerely intended for the Service of the Publick, ſo it is entirely ſubmitted to their Cenſure. As to any Miſtakes which may be obſerv'd in this Paper, I ſhall never concern my ſelf to juſtify, but ſhall freely acknowledge them. Since I ſhall equally attain my End : If I provoke ſome abler Hand to ſet the World right in their Notions concerning Treaſon. Or if I perſuade one honeſt Man, who has been deceived, to believe this almoſt ſelf evident Propoſition, *That, when it is the Act of the Supreme Power, whoever deſerves to Die, Dies juſtly.*

FINIS.